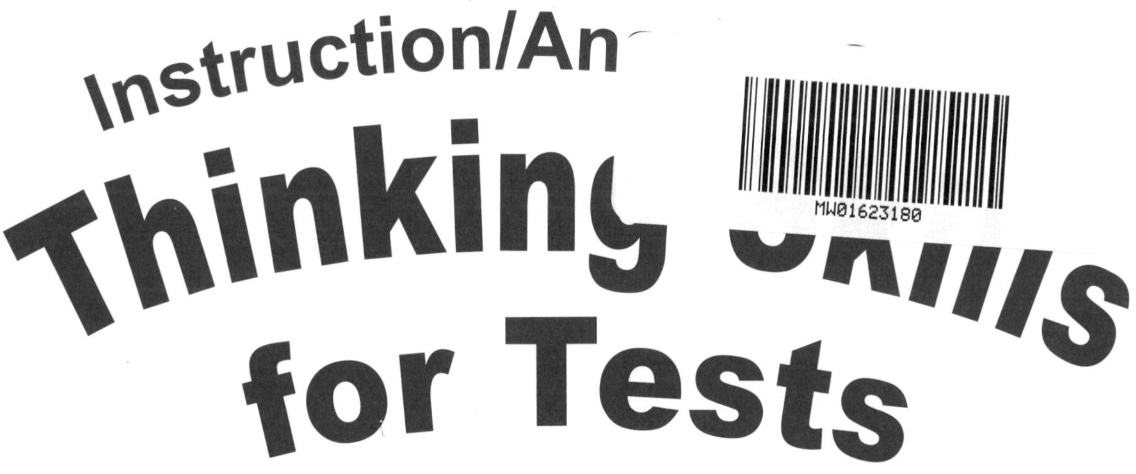

Early Learning

Thinking Skills for Tests products available in print or eBook form.

Early Learning (PreK-2)

Upper Elementary (Grades 3-5)

Written by

Robin MacFarlane, Ph.D.

Graphic Design by

Scott Slyter

THE CRITICAL THINKING CO.™

www.CriticalThinking.com

Phone: 800-458-4849 • Fax: 541-756-1758

1991 Sherman Ave., Suite 200 • North Bend • OR 97459

ISBN 978-1-60144-270-3

Printed in China by Shanghai Chenxi Printing Co., Ltd. (Dec. 2018)

TABLE OF CONTENTS

Introduction

All standardized tests measure the ability to think carefully and critically. Children can benefit from practicing critical thinking skills in a test-taking format because it enables them to give their best performance on any type of test they might take. Parents, teachers, schools, and agencies that administer tests all benefit when children perform to the best of their ability on any test that is administered to them.

Thinking Skills for Tests helps children do their best on tests by providing them with an opportunity to recognize how the critical thinking skills they already possess can be applied to a test. *Thinking Skills for Tests* presents nine thinking skills (see table of contents) that form the base of both verbal and nonverbal reasoning and logic. In the process of practicing these nine basic thinking skills, children will have the opportunity to practice listening and following directions throughout the book. They will be able to discuss answers to assure them that they're thinking carefully, and to answer questions even when the answer is uncertain and the question is difficult. This practice can build confidence, reduce anxiety, and remove obstacles that can hinder children from performing their best on tests.

Thinking Skills for Tests was prepared following ethical guidelines provided by the American Psychological Association and the National Council on Measurement in Education. The content bears no strong resemblance to any actual assessment or specific items from any assessment. Children who practice with *Thinking Skills for Tests* may perform better on standardized tests than they would without this practice, but their test scores will not rise beyond their actual ability levels.

Thinking Skills for Tests provides practice in the broad domain of critical thinking, and as such, these skills apply to a variety of standardized tests.

Administration

As a guideline, *Thinking Skills for Tests* is appropriate for children in advanced PreK through second grade.

Thinking Skills for Tests is divided into two books:

1. Workbook for children that covers nine critical thinking skills
2. Instruction/Answer Guide for teachers and parents that gives instructions that correspond to and explain the skills presented in the Workbook

Tips about the Instruction/Answer Guide:

- The question to be read verbatim appears in yellow boxes, followed by a script for discussion that appears in regular type.
- The script for discussion also can be read verbatim, or used only as a general guide. This script gives children feedback about why their answers are correct, or, if incorrect, how they can think about questions in order to get the correct answer. The script for discussion ensures that children understand each question's underlying concept.
- Because research shows that praising children for persistence predicts better academic and test performance, encouragement of persistence is part of the script.
- The correct answer choice is pictured with a circle underneath it marked in red.
- Words that appear in ALL CAPITALS should be read aloud SLOWLY for emphasis.
- The peach-colored boxes are for the parent/teacher and should not be read aloud.

Thinking Skills for Tests is a systematic method of practicing critical thinking in a test-taking format that can build children's confidence and skill knowledge. It is not designed to be scored or used as an indicator of academic or test performance.

Section I
Listening

Listening is a highly important academic skill. To listen effectively, a child needs to hear, remember, and understand the information that's being taught. Visual cues, and sometimes even tactile cues, can help children to better understand spoken information. Although older children can rely on written information in academic settings, younger children primarily rely on spoken information. This is why tests for older children are administered mostly through written information, but tests for younger children are usually administered via spoken information.

This section can help children use the listening skills they already have and build confidence in applying them to a test-like format. Children will be expected to remember brief stories, and this expectation cues them to listen attentively in a way that can help them do their best on tests.

We're going to be doing some thinking work together. There will be stories to remember and puzzles to solve. If you aren't sure of what to do, I'll help you.

1.

We'll start with number 1. Look at the four pictures. Which one of them is something that you use to WRITE? It's a pencil. You should have a pencil right now. If you don't, let's get one!

Now, see the little circle underneath the picture of the pencil? Each picture has a circle underneath it. I want you to mark the circle that's underneath the PENCIL. When you do that, you're telling me that the pencil is your answer to my question. Now, if you want to change your mind, you can erase the mark and fill in another circle. I want you to practice changing your mind. So, let's pretend that the question is different.

Here's the different question. Ready? Which one of these things do you use to help you EAT? So now what do you do? Erase the mark under the pencil and mark the circle under the SPOON.

2.

Number 2 has pictures of four things that Mrs. Smith wanted to buy at the grocery store: grapes, eggs, bread, and apples. She came home with three of the things: the GRAPES, BREAD, and APPLES. Mark the circle under the item she forgot to buy.

Let's talk about what Mrs. Smith wanted to buy to be sure that you got it right. We know that she wanted to buy four things: grapes, eggs, bread and apples. But she came home with only the grapes, bread, and apples. What did she forget? The eggs. Mark the circle under the eggs if you haven't already.

3.

Number 3 has a picture of two ponies. I'm going to tell you a story about them. Listen very carefully, and remember the story, because I'm going to ask you questions about the story later.

These ponies have been waiting for summertime to come, and they're excited that it's finally here. Some children from a school are coming by for their school picnic, and the ponies are wondering what they'll see the children play with at the picnic.

The first pony says, "I love things that can go up in the air like balls and kites. I hope the children will FLY A KITE at the picnic."

The second pony says, "I love it when kids ride around on things like skateboards and scooters. I hope that someone brings a SCOOTER to the picnic."

Turn the page, and I'll ask you questions about the story.

4.

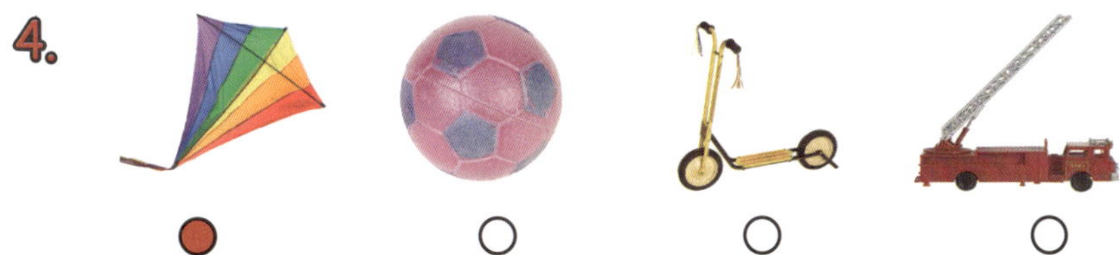

In number 4, mark the circle under the picture that shows what the FIRST pony hopes the children will play with at the picnic. You might not remember, but take a guess even if you're not sure.

If you're asked to repeat the story say the following: I can't repeat the story right now, but just do your best to answer the questions. Later on, I'll tell you the story again and you'll have another chance to answer the questions.

5.

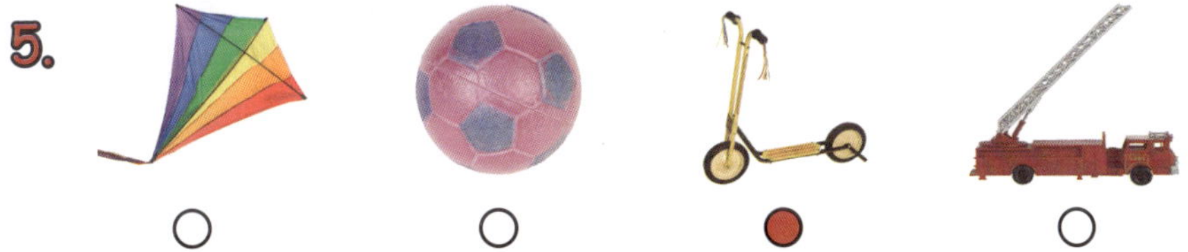

In number 5, mark the circle under the picture that shows what the SECOND pony hopes that the children will bring to the picnic.

Now, I'm going to read the story again and you'll be able to see how much you remembered. If you want, you can erase your answers and change them. Here's the story again.*

Now, you can change your answers if you want. It's okay if you don't get the answers right the first time. What's important is that you stick with it, do your best to listen, and change your answer if you listen better the second time.

Repeat the story from page 2.

Number 6 has a picture of two dogs. Now let me tell you a story about them.

These dogs are watching some kids playing! The first dog says, "I hope that little GIRL who's eating the ICE CREAM will come over and play with us."

The second dog says, "That BOY looks like he's having fun DANCING. I'm not going to wait for anyone to come over. I'm running over there right now and dancing with him."

Turn the page and I'll ask you questions about the story.

7.

In number 7, mark the circle under the picture that shows who the FIRST dog would like to play with.

You might not remember, but take a guess even if you're not sure.

If you're asked to repeat the story say the following: I can't repeat the story right now, but just do your best to answer the questions. Later on, I'll tell you the story again and you'll have another chance to answer the questions.

8.

In number 8, mark the circle under the picture that shows who the SECOND dog wants to play with.

I'm going to read the story again and you'll be able to see how much you remembered. If you want, you can erase your answers and change them. Here's the story again.*

Now, you can change your answers if you want.

**Repeat the story from page 3.*

You've completed the essential exercises in the Listening section. Continue with the last exercises in this section only if the previous ones were easily completed.

It's hard work sometimes to pay attention and listen. Keep going!

9.

The last story is about the dogs in number 9. Ready for the story?

The family that these dogs live with is having a party today. These dogs are trying to behave themselves as best they can at the party. They see lots of delicious food that they would just love to eat. One family rule is that the dogs cannot eat any food on the table. But if someone drops food on the floor, they can eat it!

The first dog says, "I see someone reaching for a piece of CHOCOLATE CAKE. I hope they drop it!"

The second dog says, "I hope that the little girl who's eating that HAMBURGER is very clumsy!

The third dog says, "Oh look, someone's holding a piece of CARROT CAKE! I hope it slips!"

Turn the page and I'll ask you questions about the story.

10.

In number 10, mark the circle under the picture of the food that the SECOND dog hopes will fall on the floor. I'm asking about the food the SECOND dog wants. Take a guess if you're not sure.

If you're asked to repeat the story say the following: I can't repeat the story right now, but just do your best to answer the questions. Later on, I'll tell you the story again and you'll have another chance to answer the questions.

11.

In number 11, mark the circle under the picture of the food that the FIRST dog hopes will fall on the floor.

12.

In number 12, mark the circle under the picture of the food that the THIRD dog hopes will fall on the floor.

I'm going to read the story again and you'll be able to see how much you remembered. If you want, you can erase your answers and change them. Here's the story again.*

Now, you can change your answers if you want.

**Repeat the story from page 5.*

Section II

Classifying Objects and Concepts

If you've ever watched *Sesame Street*, you may have seen a segment where a character sings "one of these things is not like the others," and shows some things (e.g., a shoe, a boot, a sock, and a hat), and asks children to figure out which thing doesn't belong. What children are doing (without realizing it) is deciding what similar details comprise the category (e.g., things that go on my feet) and classifying which thing doesn't belong (e.g., the hat).

In this section, children start by classifying objects based on superficial qualities (e.g., color), then begin to classify based on more sophisticated concepts. This section encourages children to explain why their choice does not belong and gives a format to do so logically, i.e., "the one that doesn't belong is . . . and the others are . . ." When children explain what the category is, and what distinguishes what is not in the category, they show that they can make careful decisions.

We're going to be looking at groups of things. You're going to choose the thing that DOESN'T belong. Look for the thing that is most different. After you choose the thing which doesn't belong, we will talk about WHY the thing you've chosen is NOT like the others. I'll help you.

1\. 

In number 1, mark the circle under the picture of the animal that is NOT like the others.

Why that one? Let's try saying it this way: The one that doesn't belong is what color? It is white. The others are black.

I want to tell you something important that you might already know. Do you think that the mouse could be the right answer?

The mouse could be the right answer because it's small, and the other animals are bigger. BUT even though the mouse could be right, the BEST answer is still the white dog. Even though the mouse is smaller than the others, it is only a little smaller than the squirrel so the white dog is the MOST different. Mark the circle under the white dog if you haven't already.

2.

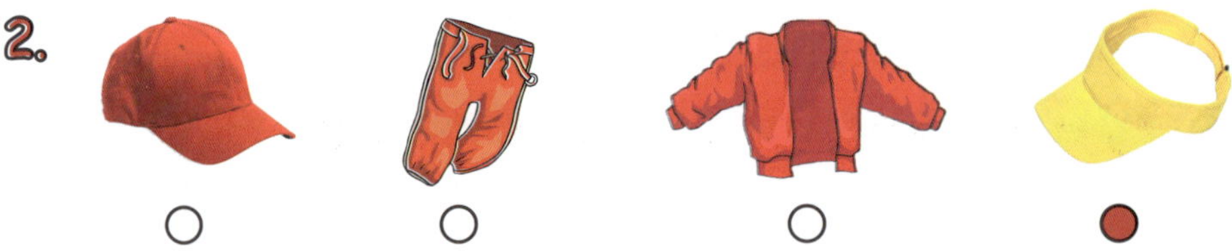

In number 2, mark the circle under the picture that is not like the others.

Let's go through the choices together and talk about the colors. Three pictures are red and one is yellow. The one that doesn't belong is YELLOW and the others are RED. The yellow visor is the thing that's the MOST different. You can change your answer if you've thought carefully and changed your mind.

3.

In number 3, mark the circle under the picture that's not like the others.

Let's look at the SHAPE of each of these things. Three shapes are circles (round) and one is a cube (square). The one that's most different is the cube.

Do you think that the purple plum could be the right answer? The plum could be the right answer. The plum isn't really round, but the cube is the most different.

4.

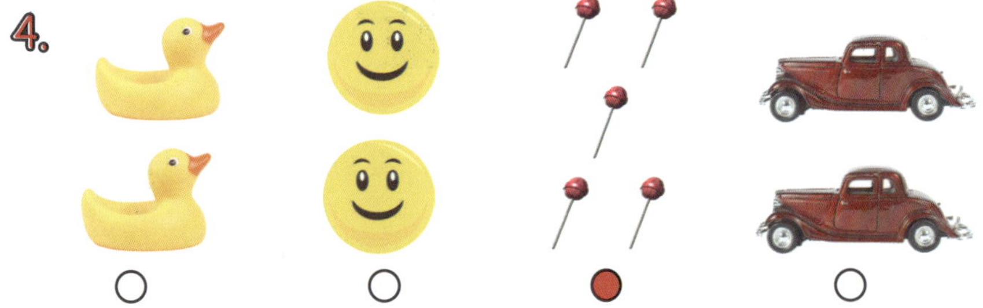

Now we're on number 4. Mark the circle under the picture that's not like the others.

What is the difference about the pictures? It can't be color because two are yellow and two are red. So, let's COUNT how many things are in each picture. The one that doesn't belong shows five things. The others show two things.

I don't expect you to know all the answers, especially when questions are hard, but I do like it when you think carefully.

5.

In number 5, mark the circle under the picture that's NOT like the others.

Let's go through the pictures together. Let's look at each of them and the way they're standing: backwards, forwards, or sideways. The one that doesn't belong is facing sideways. The others are facing backwards.

Do you think that the elephant could be the right answer? The elephant could be right. The elephant doesn't belong because it's bigger than the others. But even though the elephant could be right, the best answer is still the boy who is facing sideways. That boy is the MOST different. Go ahead and mark the circle under that boy if you haven't already.

6.

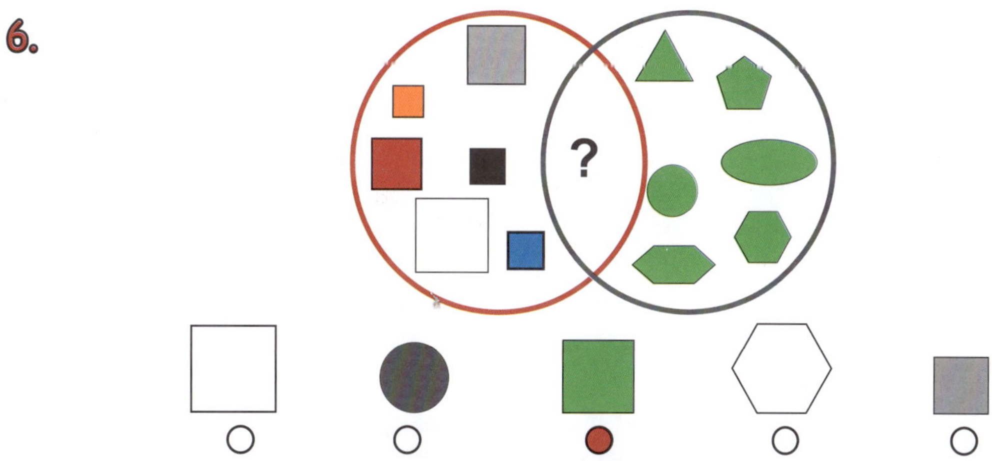

Number 6 is a different kind of activity. In the red circle, there are squares. All the squares are different colors. In the black circle, there are a lot of different shapes. But the shapes have one thing in common. What is it? They're all green.

Mark the circle under the shape that should go where the question mark is.

In the red circle, they're all squares. In the black circle, they're all green. So we're looking for a square that's green. Go ahead and mark the circle under the green square if you haven't already. You took your time, and thought carefully about things. Good job.

You've completed the essential exercises in The Classifying Objects and Concepts section. Continue with the remaining exercises only if the previous ones were completed with ease.

7.

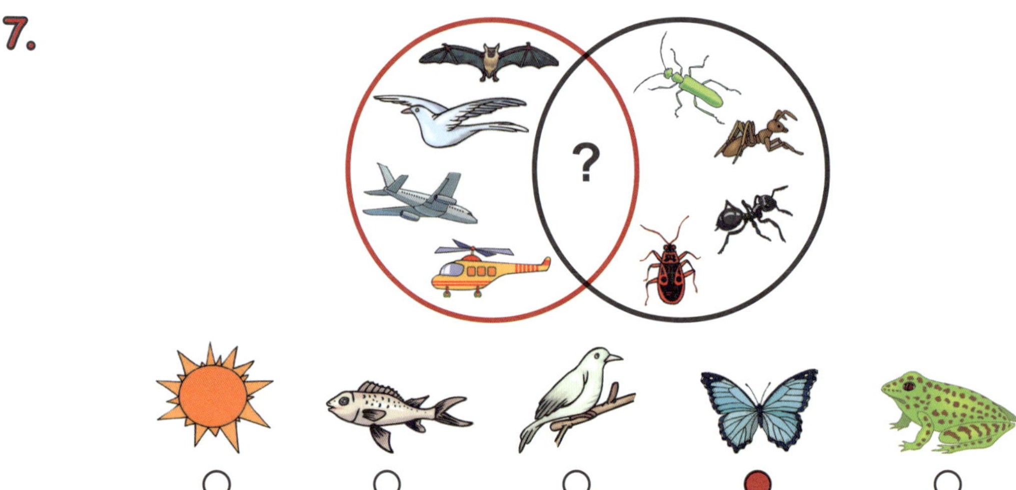

In number 7, mark the circle under the picture that should go where the question mark is.

Let's look at everything in the red circle. What are all these things doing? They are all flying. In the black circle, they are all different types of insects.

So, which one of the pictures can fly AND is an insect?

8.

Now look at the animals in number 8. Go ahead and mark the circle under the animal that's NOT like the others.

Let's look at each of the animals. What are they doing? The one that doesn't belong, is standing still. The others are running.

9.

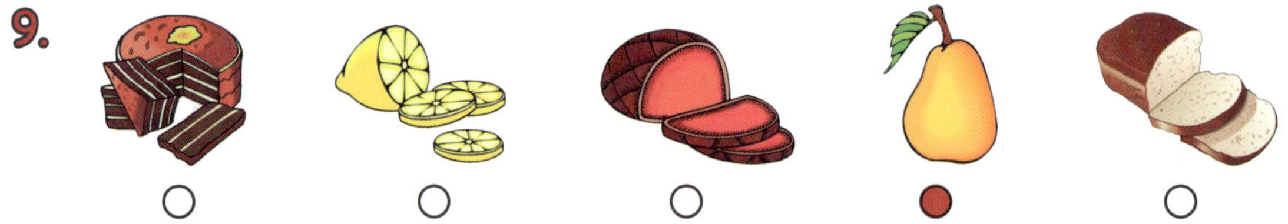

Let's move on to number 9. Mark the circle under the picture that's not like the others.

Let's look at each picture and then we'll be able to figure out which one is not like the others. The one that doesn't belong is a food that's in one piece. The others are foods cut into slices.

Good. Some of these will be easy for you, but some will be more difficult. The more difficult ones may take more time to answer. What's important is that you stick with it and keep trying.

10.

In number 10, mark the circle under the instrument that doesn't belong.

Let's look at each instrument and what part of the body you use to play it. You use your mouth to play all the instruments except the guitar.

11.

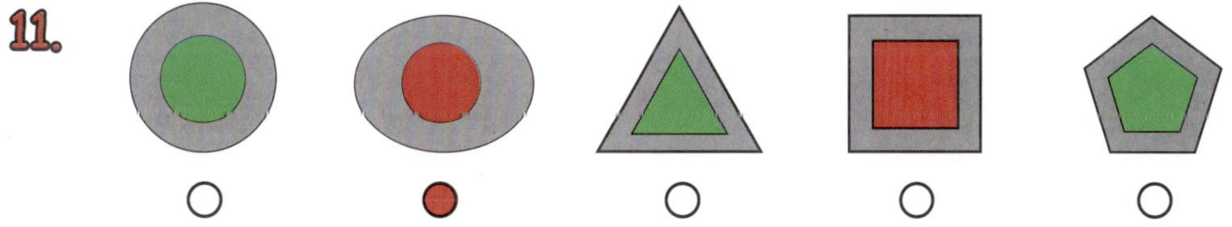

Now look at the shapes in number 11. Mark the circle under the shape that doesn't belong.

Look at each shape to see if the shape on the outside matches the shape on the inside. The one that doesn't belong has a circle inside and an oval outside. The others have the same shape inside and outside.

12.

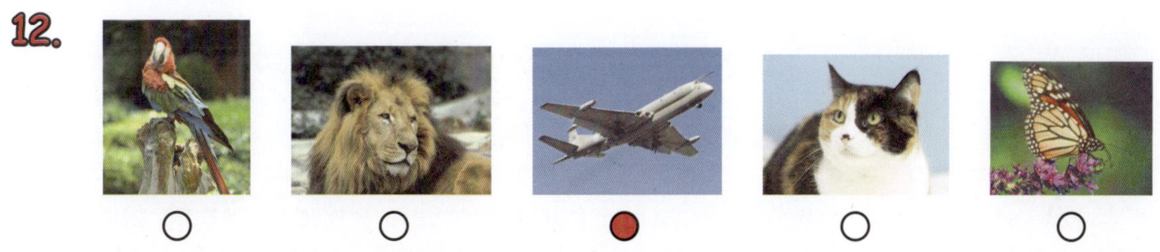

Number 12 is the last one, and it's a little challenging. Mark the circle under the picture that is not like the others.

Let's look at each picture and decide if it is alive and can eat and grow. The one that doesn't belong is not alive, doesn't eat, and can't grow. The others are all alive.

Section III

Building Vocabulary Through the Process of Elimination

Sometimes children will not answer a question, or will answer randomly, if they do not know something absolutely for sure, or if the answer is not immediately known or obvious. It is important that children feel comfortable in figuring out things that are not immediately known and also feel comfortable making a reasonable guess. One of the primary ways to do this is to rely on the process of elimination.

The first exercise in this section introduces children to the process of elimination. Starting with question number 2, children will use this skill to define words, many which they have probably never heard before. When children hear a word that is unfamiliar, it can make them feel anxious, especially when they are asked to define that word. But when they use the process of elimination, they will gain experience figuring out something that is unknown, which not only builds a thinking skill, but also enables children to feel confident using that skill.

There may be times in this book when you don't know the right answer. Sometimes you will have to guess.

1.

Right now, we're going to play a guessing game called "Who's Buddy?" One of the pets here is named Buddy. You have to listen to figure out which pet is Buddy.

I'm going to tell you something about Buddy. Buddy is NOT a big animal. He can live inside a home and doesn't have to live in a barn. Put an X over the picture that CANNOT be Buddy. Buddy is not big, so he can live inside a home. Think about the inside of your home. Which of these animals is so BIG that he could never live inside your home? The horse cannot be Buddy. Put an X over the horse if you haven't done it already. Good!

Now I'm going to tell you some more about Buddy. Buddy can get wet, but he is NOT wet all the time. Put an X over the pet who cannot be Buddy. Even though Buddy can get wet, one of these pets is wet ALL THE TIME. In fact, this pet is so wet that it lives in water. Which animal needs to be wet all the time? Buddy does NOT need to be wet all the time. The fish cannot be Buddy. Cross out the fish.

Are you ready to cross out another pet? Buddy has SOFT FUR. Put an X over the pet that cannot be Buddy. If you were going to pet these three animals, which ones do you think would feel soft? The dog and the cat have soft fur, but the turtle has a hard shell. So Buddy cannot be the turtle. Cross out the turtle.

Here's the last thing you need to know about Buddy. After you know this, you'll be able to mark the circle under the pet that is Buddy. Ready? Buddy's fur is ALL WHITE. The cat's fur is black, gray, and white. But the dog is all white. Put an X over the cat if you haven't done it already. Now, we've figured out who's Buddy! Go ahead and mark the circle under Buddy.

2.

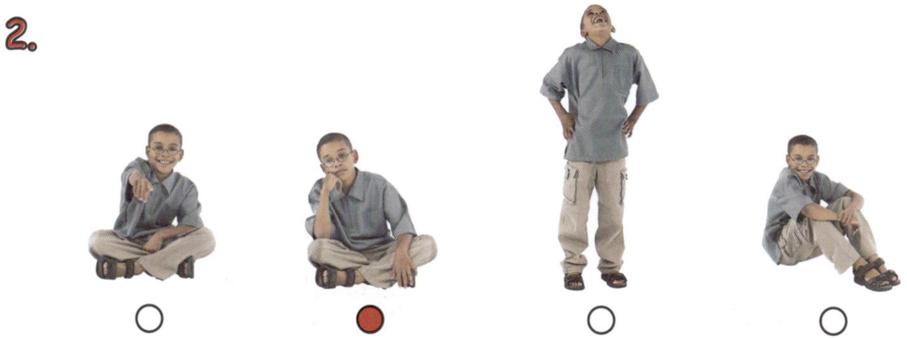

The pictures in number 2 are of a boy named Derrick. He really wanted to go outside and play, but his mom told him that he couldn't. Derrick was MOPING after his mom said he couldn't go outside and play. Mark the circle under the picture that shows Derrick MOPING.

MOPING is something a person does when he or she is disappointed and a little sad. In the second picture, Derrick looks kind of sad. But in the other pictures, he looks happy. If we cross out all the pictures where he looks happy, we have the picture where he's moping. Go ahead and mark under the picture where Derrick is moping. If you made a mistake, erase it, and mark the circle under the second picture.

3.

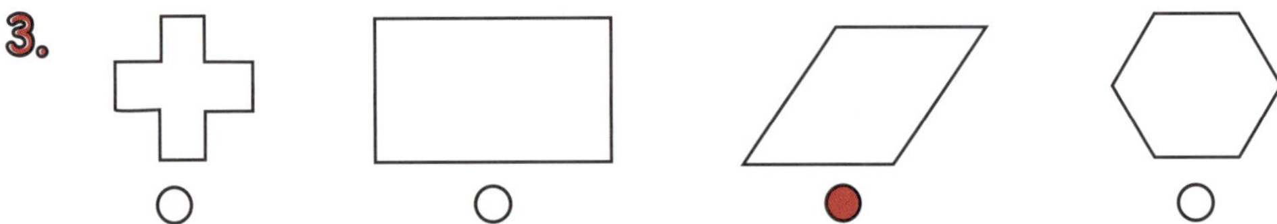

Now let's move on to number 3. I want you to mark the circle under the shape that is a RHOMBUS. Here's a clue: a RHOMBUS is a shape with four sides.

We know that a rhombus is a shape with four sides. So, we can cross out the first and last shape, because these have more than four sides.

That leaves us with the two shapes in the middle. We know that one of these shapes is a rectangle. So, that means that the other shape with four sides is the rhombus. Something interesting that you might already know is that a rhombus always has four sides that are the same length.

4.

Now let's move on to number 4. I want you to find the EXCAVATOR. Here's a clue: an EXCAVATOR is a type of truck. Mark the circle under the EXCAVATOR.

You may have already got it right, but let's go ahead and figure it out together. We know that an excavator is a truck. But here's another clue. It's a type of truck that digs into the ground. There are two things that are not trucks. One is the shovel and the other is the van. Let's cross them out.

Now, one of these trucks is a dump truck and doesn't dig into the ground. The other one, with the big shovel on it, is the excavator. Go ahead and mark the circle under the excavator, if you haven't already. Remember you can change your answer if you've thought carefully and changed your mind.

5.

Now, we're going to move on to number 5. Ready? A KUMQUAT is a type of fruit. Mark the circle under the KUMQUAT.

We know that a kumquat is a fruit. There are two things here that are not fruit. You can eat fruit, but you better not eat a hat or a lizard. Let's cross them out. We have two choices left. You already know what bananas are. So a kumquat must be the other one, the last one.

You've completed the essential exercises in the Building Vocabulary Through the Process of Elimination section. Continue with the remaining exercises only if the previous ones were easily completed.

6.

Look at the pictures in number 6. BINOCULARS are something you look through to make things that are far away appear closer. Mark the circle under the child who has BINOCULARS.

We know that binoculars are something you look through. There is one picture here where a child is not looking through anything, and it's the picture where the boy is with his doctor. Let's cross it out.

Now, which one of the other pictures looks like it can make things that are far away seem close? The first picture won't work. Let's cross it out.

Now, one of the other two pictures shows a child who has binoculars. Which one do you think it is? One of these is of a child with sunglasses. So the child with binoculars must be the other one. Go ahead and mark the circle under the picture of the child with binoculars.

7.

Now we're on number 7. A MANATEE is an animal that lives in the ocean. Mark the circle under the picture of the MANATEE.

We know that a manatee is an animal that lives in the ocean. There are two animals here that live on the land and not in the ocean. These are the llama and the buffalo. Let's cross them out.

Now, a manatee is one of the other two. Which one do you think it is? One of these animals, the last animal, is a dolphin. So a manatee must be the other one, the first one. Go ahead and mark the circle under the manatee, if you haven't already.

8.

Look at the pictures in number 8. A DINGO is a wild animal that looks like a dog. Mark the circle under the DINGO.

Let's cross out all the animals that do not look like dogs. Cross out the bear and cat. Now cross out the dog that is not wild. The dingo is the only picture left.

9.

Now we're on number 9. A DIRIGIBLE is a type of air transportation. Mark the circle under the DIRIGIBLE.

We know that a dirigible is a type of air transportation. There are two things here that are not air transportation. One is the balloon, because you cannot ride in this type of balloon! And the other is the car, because even though you can ride in a car, it doesn't go in the air and so isn't air transportation. Let's cross out the car and the balloon. Now, a dirigible is one of the other two. Which one do you think it is?

One of these things you already know is an airplane. So a dirigible must be the other one, the first one. A dirigible is also called a "blimp."

10.

The last one is number 10. An ORCHID is a flower known for its uncommon shape and color. Mark the circle under the ORCHID.

We know that an orchid is a flower, so cross out the pictures that are not flowers. Only two pictures are left and they are both flowers. One of the flowers that is left is a dandelion, so we know that can't be an orchid. Cross out the dandelion. The orchid is left.

Section IV
Relating Concepts

Relating concepts requires children to think about how things relate to other things. Children will be asked to select, for example, something that is the tallest, or something that is in the middle of other things. In addition, children will be asked to integrate concepts, that is, to think about more than one concept at the same time. For example, children will be asked not only to select what is tallest, but also to identify a picture where what is tallest is also in the middle. Complicated logical thinking, and following a complicated set of directions, usually involves relating concepts. Here, those concepts are broken down so that children will have the opportunity to master the idea of one relational concept, and then integrate it with others.

I want you to keep listening carefully, just like you've already done. Some of these questions might be easy, but some might be hard. The important thing is that you take your time and think about each question carefully. We'll discuss some of these questions as we go through them to make sure you understand everything.

1.

Here's the first question in this section. Look at the children in number 1. Mark the circle under the child who is the TALLEST.

It's the last boy.

2.

In number 2, there are four pictures of children. Mark the circle under the picture that shows the TALLEST child from exercise number 1 in the MIDDLE.

Let's look at the first two pictures. Is the tallest child in either of these two pictures? He's not here! But he is in the last two pictures. So let's look only at the last two pictures. Which one shows the tallest child in the middle of two other children? He should be in-between two other children who are shorter than he is.

3.

Look at the pictures in number 3. Mark the circle under the picture that shows the tallest child in the middle with a dog right NEXT TO him.

There are a lot of things to think about here. First, we want to find the picture where the tallest child is in the middle, just like you did before. The first two pictures show the tallest child in the middle. Let's circle them, because one of them is our answer.

Next, we want to find the picture where the tallest child is in the middle AND there's a dog right next to him. Which one of the pictures that you've circled shows a dog right next to the tallest child? When you find that picture, you'll know the answer.

4.

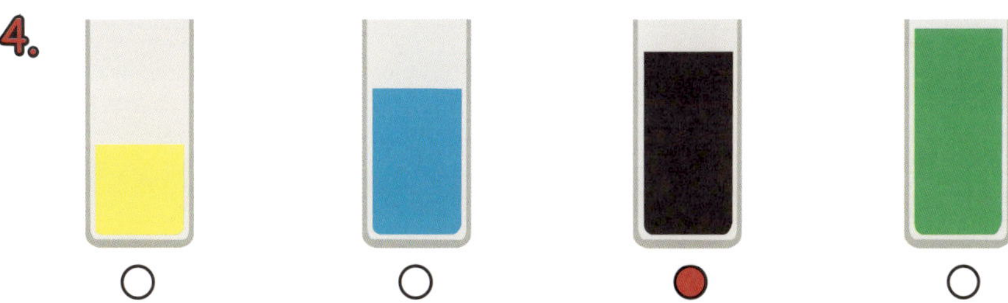

In number 4, there are four glasses of water. The water in each glass is a different color. One is yellow, one's blue, one's black, and one's green. Mark the circle under the glass that has the water that is the DARKEST COLOR.

It's the third glass, because black is the darkest of all the colors.

5.

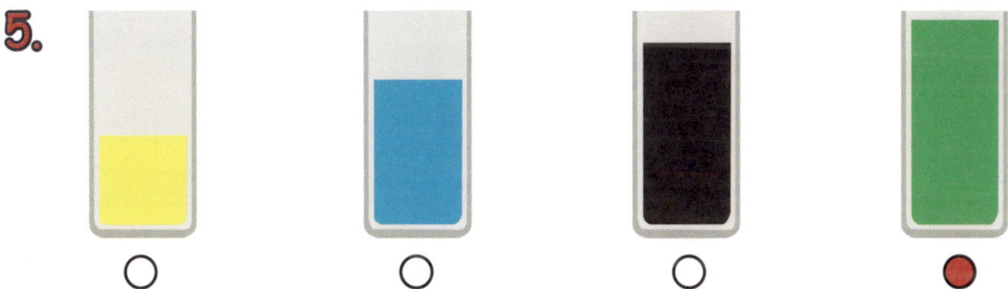

Now we're on question number 5, looking at the same glasses of water. This time I want you to do something different. This time I want you to mark the circle under the glass that is the FULLEST.

The last glass is the fullest. Now, you know two important things. You know which glass has the DARKEST WATER, and you also know which one is the FULLEST.

6.

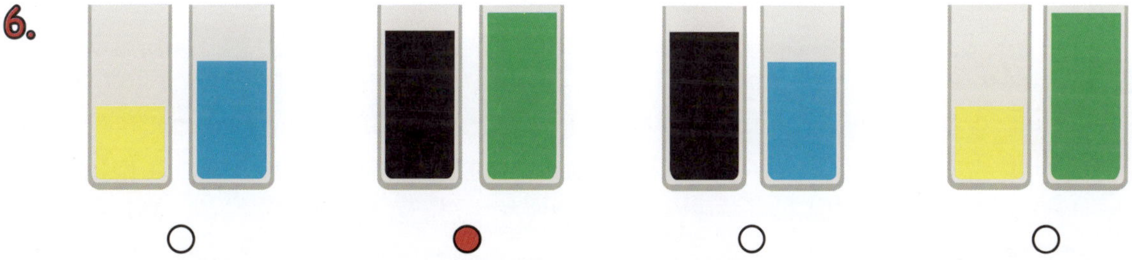

In number 6, I want you to mark the circle under the picture that has BOTH the DARKEST WATER and the FULLEST glass.

The second glasses are correct.

7.

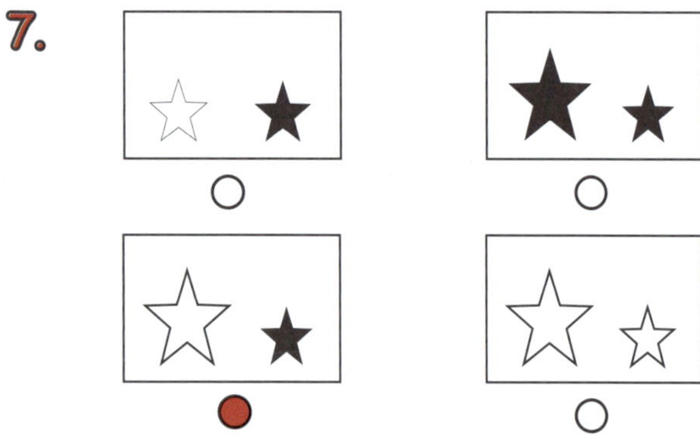

Now look at number 7. There are four pictures here, and all the pictures have two stars. I want you to mark the circle under the picture that has a BIG WHITE STAR AND A SMALL BLACK STAR.

There are lots of things to remember. I'm going to tell you one thing at a time and then you'll know the answer for sure.

The picture I'm thinking of has one big white star in it. Let's circle all the pictures that have one big white star. This picture has one big white star, AND ALSO one SMALL BLACK star. Which one is it?

8.

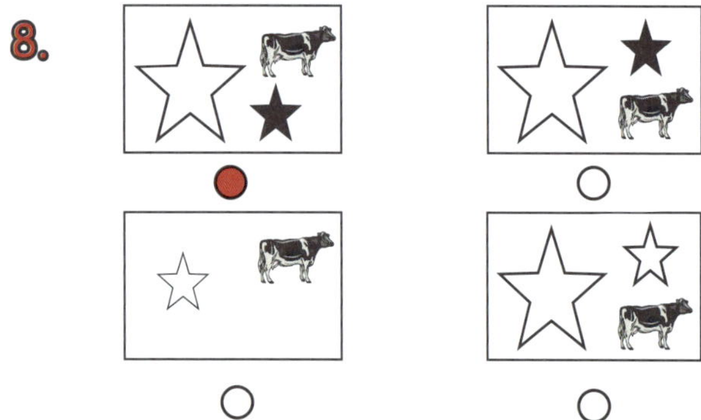

In number 8, there are four pictures, but this time, there's a cow in them. I want you to mark the circle under the picture that has a BIG WHITE STAR NEXT TO A COW THAT IS STANDING OVER A SMALL BLACK STAR. Can you find it?

I'm going to tell you one thing at a time and then you'll know the answer for sure.

The picture I'm thinking of has one big white star in it. Let's circle all the pictures with one big white star.

Here's the second thing: The picture I'm thinking of has a cow standing over a small black star. That means that the cow is on top of a small black star. Which one is it? Remember, you can change your answer if you've thought carefully and changed you mind.

You've completed the essential exercises in Relating Concepts section. Continue with the remaining exercises only if the previous ones were easily completed.

9.

In number 9, the dogs are sitting in line, waiting for a treat. The dog that's closest to the treats is first in line.

I want you to listen to what I'm going to say, and mark the circle next to the picture I'm talking about. Ready? There are FOUR dogs. The SHORTEST dog is LAST.

I'm looking for a picture with FOUR dogs in it, where the shortest dog is last. That's a lot of things to remember. Let's start by circling the pictures with four dogs. Look at the last two pictures. They both have four dogs in them. The dog that's closest to the treats is first in line. Now, mark the circle next to the picture where the SHORTEST dog is LAST, if you haven't already.

10.

In number 10, mark the circle under the picture that shows the dancer with BOTH FEET on the floor and ONE ARM lifted OVER her head.

The first thing you need to look at are the feet on the floor. Let's cross out the first one because she only has one foot on the floor.

Now, the second thing to remember is that she has only one arm lifted over her head. Which one of these shows only one arm over her head? Go ahead and mark the circle under it, if you haven't already.

11.

Now we're on number 11. Mark the circle under the picture that shows the highest part of the flying bird is its head.

Am I looking for a flying bird? I am. So, we can cross out the last bird because it's not flying. Now, I'm looking for a flying bird where its HEAD is the highest part of its body. So, which of these birds has its head higher than the rest of it? Go ahead and mark the circle under it, if you haven't already.

12.

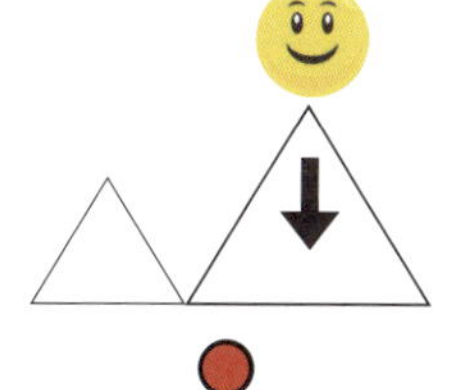

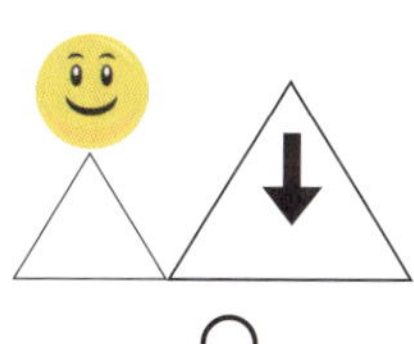

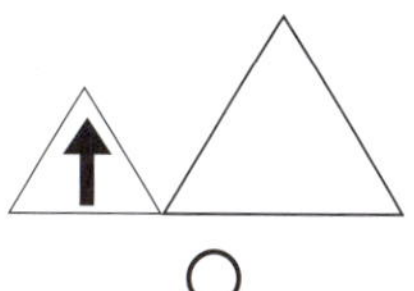

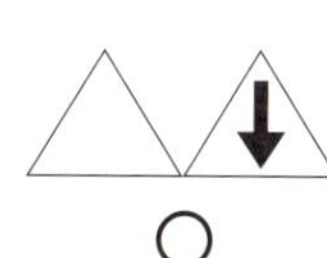

Mark the circle under the picture that shows the BIGGER triangle with an arrow inside of it pointing down and a happy face on top of it.

The first thing is that the bigger triangle has an arrow pointing down inside of it. Go ahead and circle the ones where the bigger triangle has an arrow pointing down inside of it.

The other clue is that the bigger triangle has a happy face on top of it. Now mark the circle under the picture where the bigger triangle has an arrow pointing down inside of it and a happy face on top of it.

13. 56 55 55 56

Mark the circle under the picture where numbers are the SAME size, but DIFFERENT numbers.

First, let's circle the choices where the two numbers are the same size. Second, we need to find numbers that are NOT ONLY the same size, BUT ALSO are different numbers. So, of the choices we've circled, which one has different numbers? Go ahead and mark that one if you haven't already.

14. 56 55 55 56

Now we're on the last problem. Listen to what I want you to do: Mark the circle under the picture where the numbers are DIFFERENT sizes, but they are the SAME number.

First, let's circle the choices where the two numbers are different sizes. Second, we need to find numbers that NOT ONLY are different sizes, BUT ALSO are the same number. So, of the choices we've circled, which one has the same number? Go ahead and mark that one if you haven't already. Remember you can change your answer if you've thought carefully and changed your mind.

Section V
Verbal Reasoning

Verbal reasoning requires children to make sense of spoken logic puzzles and "common sense" questions. One thing that can confuse children about logic puzzles and common sense questions is that even though there may be a "best" answer, there are often other answers that are plausible. With practice, children have the opportunity to build confidence in their ability to identify the best answer.

In this section, I'm going to be telling you some short stories and asking you questions, and you're going to be marking the circle under the right answer, just like you've been doing. Sometimes, you may not be sure of the right answer. But I want you to do your best. The most important thing is to think carefully.

1.

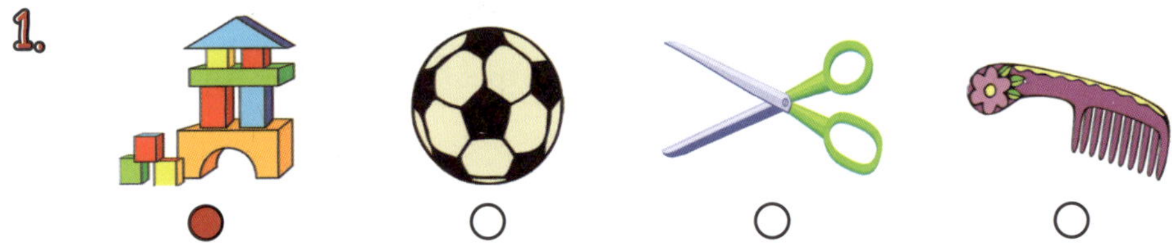

Ready? Look at the pictures in number 1. Mark the circle under the picture that shows a children's toy.

Sometimes, there's more than one right answer. Children can play with any of these things.

But, even though all these answers might be right, there is one answer that is better than the rest. There is one answer that is a toy and that grown-ups usually don't use.

The best answer is the first one, the blocks. A lot of times, grown-ups play with a soccer ball, and use scissors or a comb. Only children usually play with blocks. If a grown-up plays with blocks, usually they are playing with YOU! Go ahead and mark the circle under the block if you haven't already.

2.

Let's move on to number 2. Listen to the story: A boy named Dante went to the library. When he was at the library, he saw lots of interesting things there. When he left, he checked something out and took it home with him. Mark the circle under the thing that Dante CHECKED OUT of the library.

You can see all of these things at the library, so anything you mark might be okay. But which thing do libraries have in them that they want you to check out and take home with you? Can you take home a computer or a globe? No!

You CAN take home a pencil, but the special thing about libraries is that they have what? Books!

3.

Now we're on number 3. Listen to the story: Steven is only 1 year old, just a baby. He likes to play a musical instrument. Mark the circle under the instrument that Steven plays.

A baby might play any one of these instruments, but a baby cannot play most instruments very well at all. But there is one instrument here that a baby can play by just beating his hand on it. Which one is that?

4.

Let's move on to number 4. Listen to the story: At Astor Park Zoo, Bella is a striped animal. ALL of the zebras have names that begin with the letter "Z," like "Zelda" and "Zorro." Mark the circle under the picture that shows Bella.

We're trying to figure out which animal is Bella. We know that Bella is an animal with stripes. So let's cross out all the animals that do not have stripes.

We now know that Bella is either the zebra or the tiger. But all the zebras have names that begin with the letter Z. So which animal is Bella? The tiger.

5.

Look at the fruit in number 5. Listen to the story: Tricia and her dad are making fruit salad. They have four different fruits on the table: apples, bananas, strawberries, and watermelon. Tricia's dad has already cut up STRAWBERRIES, BANANAS, and APPLES. There's one more fruit he has to cut up to make the salad. Mark the circle under the fruit that Tricia's dad is going to cut up next.

There are a lot of things to remember about this story. You have to listen very carefully, and that's hard to do sometimes. We know that there are four fruits on the table that are going into the fruit salad, and they are the four choices. The strawberries, apples, and bananas have already been added to the salad. So the one that still needs to be added is the right answer. It's not any one of the first three, so it's the watermelon. Go ahead and mark the circle under the watermelon if you haven't already.

6.

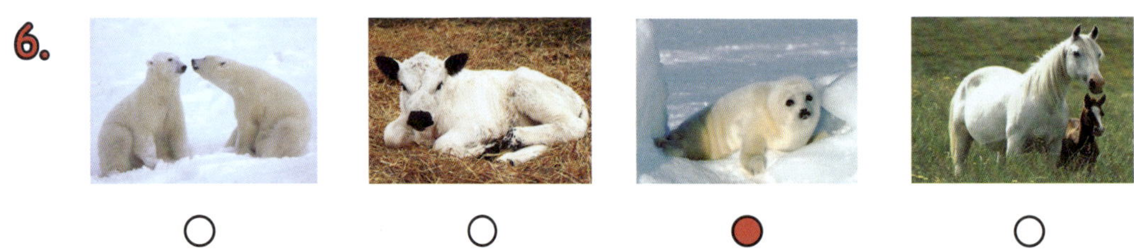

Let's move on to number 6. I'm going to tell you about an animal named Harvey and I want you to guess who he is. Listen to the story: Harvey's going to meet one of his friends later to play in the snow, but right now, he's spending time alone. Mark the circle under the picture of Harvey.

There are a lot of things to remember about the story. First, is Harvey with someone else right now, or is he all alone? He's spending time alone right now. So, we can cross out the polar bears and the baby horse that's with its mom.

Next, we know that Harvey is going to meet a friend later to play in the snow. Which animal do you think would play in the snow? Go ahead and mark the circle under the seal if you haven't already.

7.

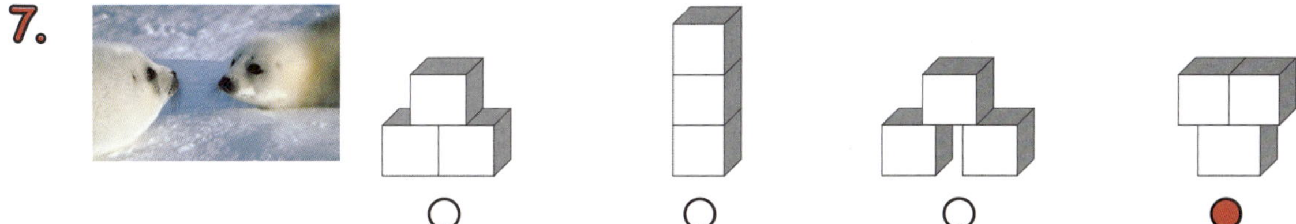

Number 7 is a story about what happened when Harvey and his friend played in the snow. Listen: They found some blocks of ice. Harvey built something with the blocks, and his friend said, "That looks like the top part is too big and will fall down!" Mark the circle under the picture of what Harvey built.

To answer this question, you have to think about building with blocks. If you build something where the top part is smaller than the bottom part, like the first and third one, it really looks like the top part will stay on there. If the bottom part is bigger than the top part, then the top part is not likely to fall over. So, we can cross out the first one and the third one.

The second one has a top part that is the same size as the bottom part. But look at the last one. What do you think of that one? I think that Harvey's friend was right when he said that the top part is too big and might fall down.

8.

Look at the pictures in number 8. These are four pictures of a boy named Josh and his dad. I'm going to tell you a story about them, and after I tell you, I want you to mark the circle under the picture that describes the story.

Ready? Listen to the story: Josh and his dad were watching a baseball game. Josh's dad was having a good time and was enjoying the game. But Josh was bored and tired and wanted to go home. Mark the circle under the picture that best describes the story.

There is one important thing to know that will help you decide which picture is right. It's about Josh and how he was feeling. Josh was feeling bored and tired and wanted to go home.

If you look at the first three pictures, you see Josh pointing, smiling, and waving his hands in the air. In the first three pictures, Josh looks like he's having a good time. But let's look at Josh in the last picture. In the last picture, do you think that Josh looks bored and tired? It seems like the last picture is the best answer.

You've completed the essential exercises in the Verbal Reasoning section. Continue with the remaining exercises only if the previous ones were easily completed.

9.

Let's move on to a story about the pictures in number 9. Listen to the story: Alex is out for a walk in the park with his mother. His mother tells him that she isn't sure which way they should go. Mark the circle under the picture of the BEST grown-up for his mother to ask for directions.

Alex's mother could ask any one of these people for directions so any one that you mark might be okay. But a lot of them look kind of busy, reading the newspaper, talking on the phone, or jogging. Which person here has a job where he is supposed to help people? It's the police officer's job to help people when they are lost, and so the police officer is the best one to ask for direction.

10.

Let's try number 10. Listen to the story: Ling went to the PETTING ZOO. Her favorite part of the day was when she got to pick up and cuddle this animal in her arms. Mark the circle under the animal that she held.

You can put your arms around any one of these animals, but there is only one animal that you can pick up and cuddle in your arms. One of these animals is small, soft, and cuddly. Let's look at each one, and decide whether or not we can pick it up and carry it, and then we'll know the answer.

11.

Number 11 is about a girl named Laura. Laura was outside on a very hot day. She saw a big garbage truck roll by. Mark the circle under the picture that shows what she might do after seeing the garbage truck.

The important thing here is to think about a garbage truck. Some kids really love seeing garbage trucks, and those kids would probably smile like Laura is smiling in the last picture. But let's think about a garbage truck. We know that they look very interesting, but let's think about what they smell like, especially on a hot day when the garbage really stinks. The best answer is the second choice that shows Laura holding her nose because something is stinky.

12.

  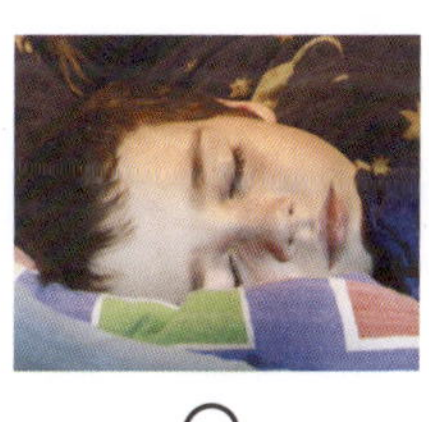 

Look at the pictures in number 12. Mark the circle under the picture of the child who is doing something that will help him to stay both HEALTHY and CLEAN.

All of these things are healthy things to do. But which of the children is not only doing something healthy, but also is doing something that will help him to be CLEAN? Let's go through them all, and decide which one of these shows a child doing something that will help him to keep clean.

13.

Let's move on to number 13. Mark the circle under the picture that shows a hungry butterfly finding what it really wanted.

If a butterfly is hungry, where can it get food? Can a butterfly get food from a book? A candle? A duck? That's all silly! Butterflies get their food from what? Flowers.

14.

Let's move on to number 14. This story is about a boy named Sean and the foods he likes and doesn't like. Listen carefully. Sean does NOT like to eat pretzels. Sean DOES LIKE to eat ice cream. However, Sean's very FAVORITE food is pizza.

Mark the circle under the picture that shows, in order, the food that Sean likes the best, then second best, and then least.

When you listen carefully, you can figure this out. I'll say it again another way. Listen: Sean's favorite food is pizza. Sean likes ice cream, but he does not like pretzels.

Which one is Sean's very favorite food? It's pizza. Which is the food that he does not like? Pretzels. Does he like ice cream at all? Yes. So, it looks like ice cream is in the middle, but pizza is first, and because he doesn't like pretzels, they're last.

15.

You're doing a great job. Now onto number 15. Listen to the story: Emma and Julie both have pets, but their pets are DIFFERENT animals. Emma's pet sings, and Julie's pet does NOT bark and does NOT purr. Mark the circle under the picture of Julie's pet.

We're trying to figure out which one of these pets is Julie's pet. This one may take more time because you have a lot of things to think about and remember. You have to remember that Emma's pet sings, and Julie's pet does not bark and does not purr.

Let's take things slowly. Emma's pet sings. So which one is Emma's pet? Remember, Julie and Emma have different pets so Julie's pet is NOT a bird. So you can cross out the bird.

Julie's pet does not bark and does not purr. So we can cross out animals that bark and purr. When we do that, we can see which pet is Julie's. Mark the circle under the rabbit if you haven't already.

Section VI
Reasoning With Analogies

Analogies teach children how relationships are similar to one another. For example, even though "dogs" generally have nothing to do with "squares," the relationship between a big dog and a little dog is like the relationship between a big square and a little square. The underlying concept is one of size.

This section covers four types of analogies that reflect:

1. change in relative degree, such as size or number (e.g., three dogs and one dog go together in the same way as three eggs and one egg),
2. part of a whole (e.g., a single rose is part of a whole bouquet),
3. change in position (e.g., a sun moving across the top of a square is like the same sun moving in the same direction at the bottom of the square),
4. and knowledge of typical functions, categories, or locations (e.g., a fish is typically found in an aquarium much like a cow is typically found in a barnyard).

Although it may be enough to simply answer the questions, discussion of the relationships can solidify clear thinking about analogies and also build confidence.

1.

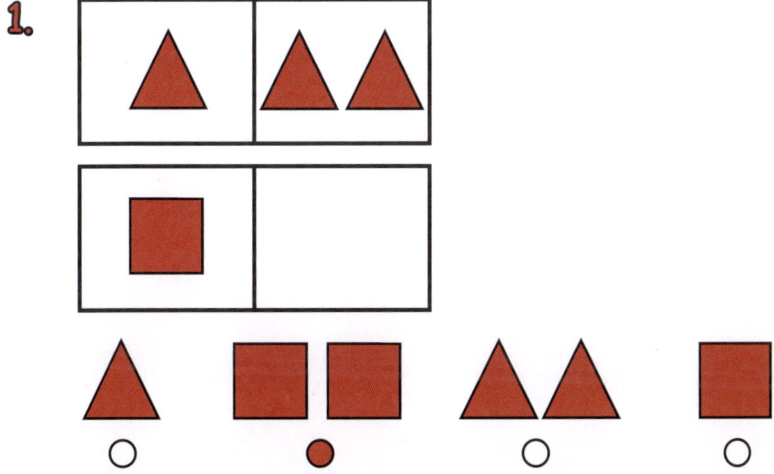

Look at the picture in number 1. This is a new type of puzzle we're going to be doing. Look at the pictures in the top boxes. There is one triangle. Right next to it, there are two triangles. One triangle and two triangles go together in a certain way.

In the bottom boxes, there is one square, and an empty box. Now look at the four pictures under the boxes. One of them belongs in the empty box. Which one is it?

It's the one with two squares. Go ahead and mark the circle under it. You see, one triangle and two triangles go together in the same way as one square and two squares.

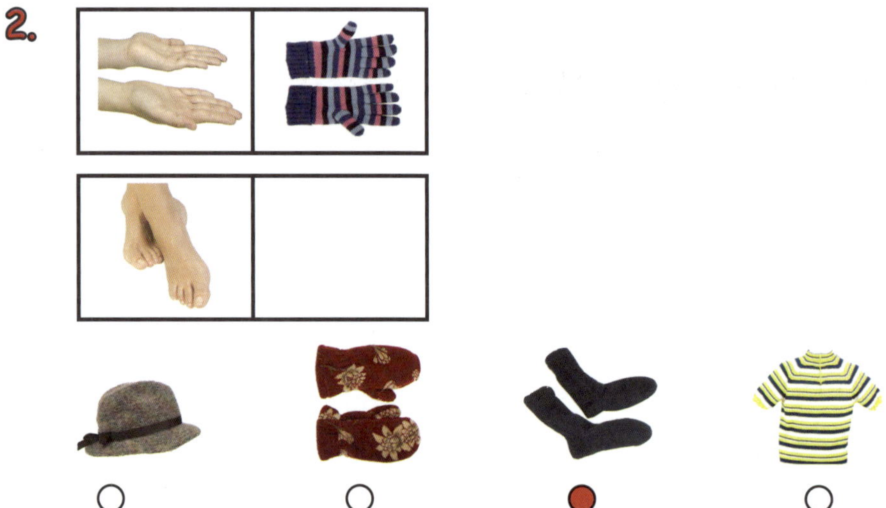

Now look at the pictures in the boxes in number 2. Mark the circle under the picture that belongs in the empty box.

In the top boxes, there's a picture of someone's hands and right next to it, there are some gloves. Hands and gloves go together in a certain way.

In the bottom boxes, there are someone's feet and an empty box. Look at the four pictures under the boxes. Which one belongs in the empty space? It's the socks.

Now, how do the hands and gloves go together? Gloves go on hands. How do the feet and socks go together? Socks go on feet. The two top pictures go together in the same way as the two bottom pictures.

We're going to do more puzzles like the ones we just did. For all of these, the pictures in the top boxes go together in a certain way. Your job is to look at the picture in the bottom box and decide what belongs in the empty space next to it.

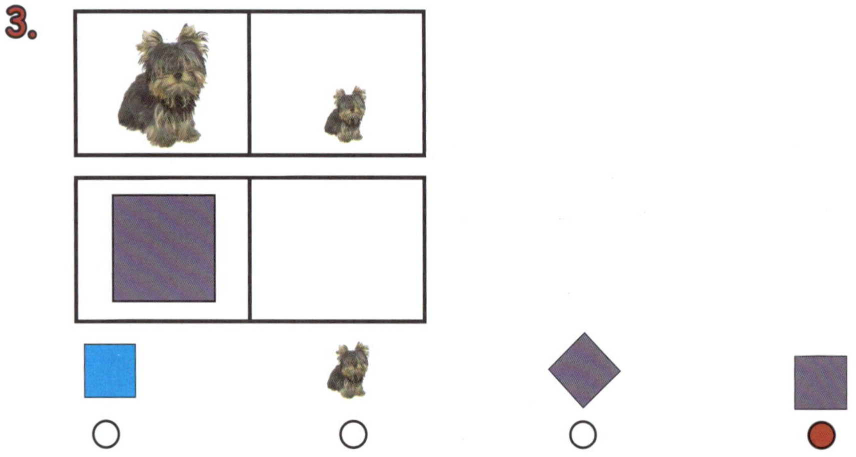

Now try number 3. Mark the circle under the picture that belongs in the empty box.

In the top boxes, there's a big dog, and then there's a dog that looks just like it, only smaller.

In the bottom boxes, there's a big purple square and an empty box. Big dog and little dog go together in the same way as what? Big purple square and little purple square. Mark the circle under the little purple square if you haven't already.

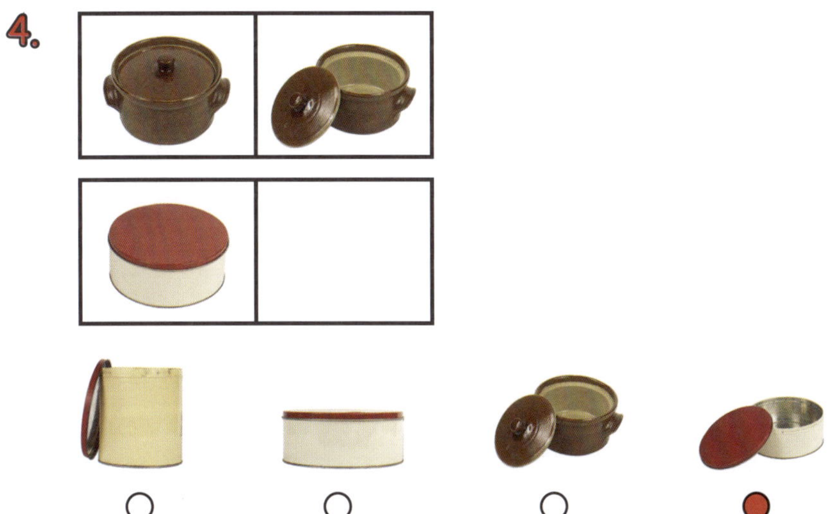

Now try number 4. Mark the circle under the picture that belongs in the empty box.

In the top boxes, there's a pot with a lid on top, and then the same pot with the lid off.

In the bottom boxes, there's a container with the lid on top and an empty box. So we're looking for the same container only with the lid off. Two of the pictures are not the same container as the container in the bottom picture so we can cross them out. Only one of the remaining pictures shows the lid off, so this is the correct answer. Remember, you can change your answer if you've thought carefully and changed your mind.

Now we're on number 5. Mark the circle under the picture that belongs in the empty box.

Let's talk about your answer. It really shows me how much you understand. In the top boxes, you see three dogs, and then one dog. Three dogs and one dog go together in the same way as three eggs and what? One egg. For both the top and the bottom boxes, first there are three, and then there is only one.

6.

Go ahead and look at number 6. Mark the circle under the picture that belongs in the empty box.

In the top boxes, there is a bunch of flowers, and then one flower. The one flower is part of the whole bunch of flowers.

In the bottom boxes, there are a bunch of balloons, and an empty box.

Another way to say this is that both the top and bottom boxes show a group of things, like flowers or balloons, and then they show one of the things in the group.

You're showing me that you know how to think through these puzzles carefully. That's great.

7.

Now we're on number 7. Mark the circle under the picture that belongs in the empty box.

In the top boxes, there's a girl standing, and then the same girl is upside down. A girl standing up and then turning upside down goes together in the same way as a letter "A" facing right-side up and then what? Turning upside down.

Another way to say this is that both the top and bottom boxes show a person or a letter facing the usual way, and then that person or letter is turned upside down.

8.

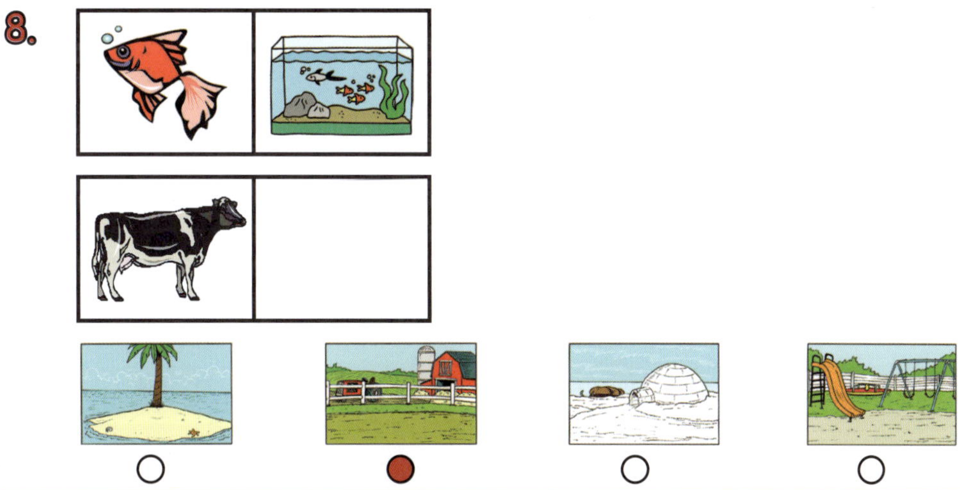

In number 8, mark the circle under the picture that belongs in the empty box.

In the top boxes, there's a fish, and the next picture shows a place where fish live. The tank is the fish's home.

In the bottom boxes, there's a cow and an empty box. Where does the cow live? Do we find cows on desert islands, or icy igloos, or playing with kids on the playground? No!

A fish and a fish tank go together in the same way as a cow and a what? A barnyard or farm.

You've completed the essential exercises in the Reasoning With Analogies section. Continue with the remaining exercises only if the previous ones were easily completed.

9.

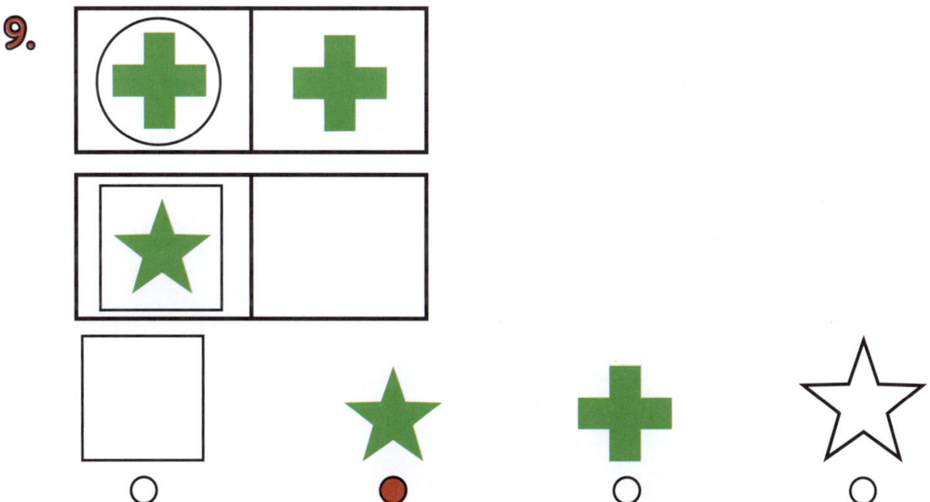

In number 9, mark the circle under the picture that goes in the empty box.

In the top boxes, there is a green cross inside of a circle, and then just the cross by itself. A cross inside a circle and then all by itself goes together in the same way as a star inside a square and then what? A star by itself.

Another way to say this is that both the top and bottom boxes show a green shape inside another shape, and then they show the shape all by itself.

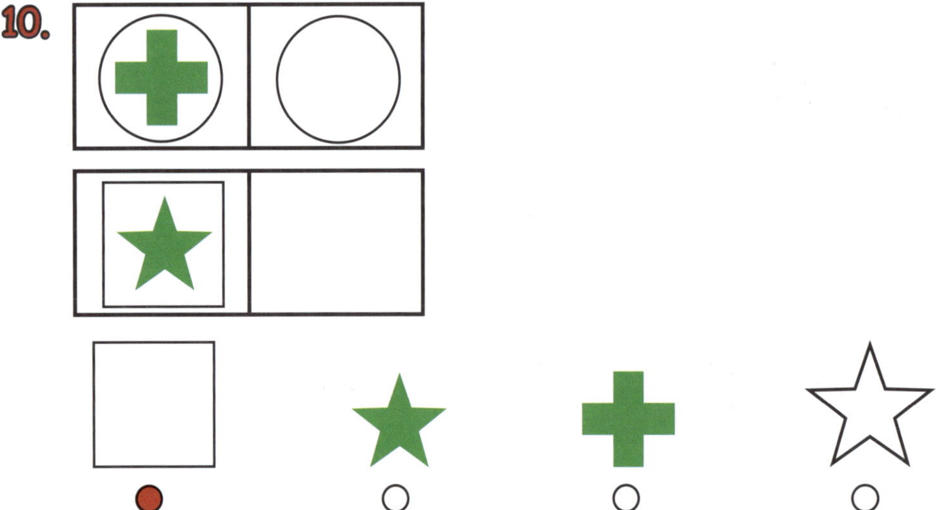

Now try number 10. Mark the circle under the picture that belongs in the empty box.

In the top boxes, there is a cross inside of a circle, and then just the circle by itself. A cross inside a circle and then the circle by itself goes together in the same way as a star inside a square and then what? A square by itself.

These kinds of puzzles may be a challenge, but stick with it and keep trying to figure it out. You're doing great at that.

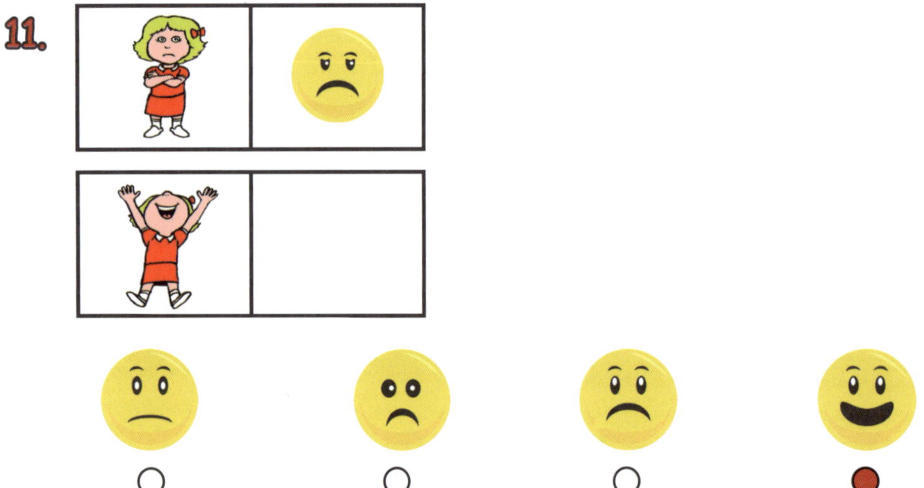

In number 11, mark the circle under the picture that belongs in the empty box

In the top boxes, there's a girl with a sad face and then another face with the same sad expression.

What does the girl on the bottom look like? She looks really, really happy. What is the face that looks really, really happy just like the girl? There are three kinds of sad faces, but the last face looks happy and most like the girl.

12.

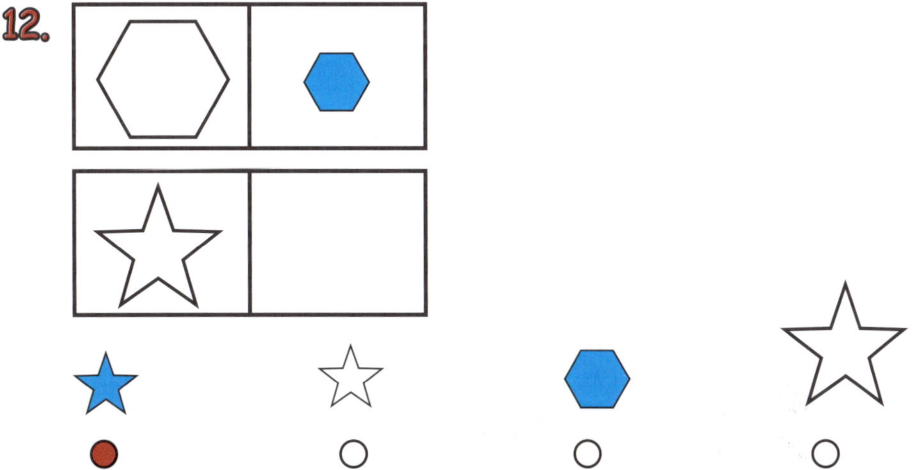

Now try number 12. Mark the circle under the picture that belongs in the empty box.

In the top boxes, there's a big shape, called a hexagon, and next to it is a smaller blue hexagon.

In the bottom boxes, there's a big star and an empty box. So we're looking for a star that looks just like it, only smaller and blue. Big hexagon and little blue hexagon go together in the same way as what? A big star and a little blue star.

13.

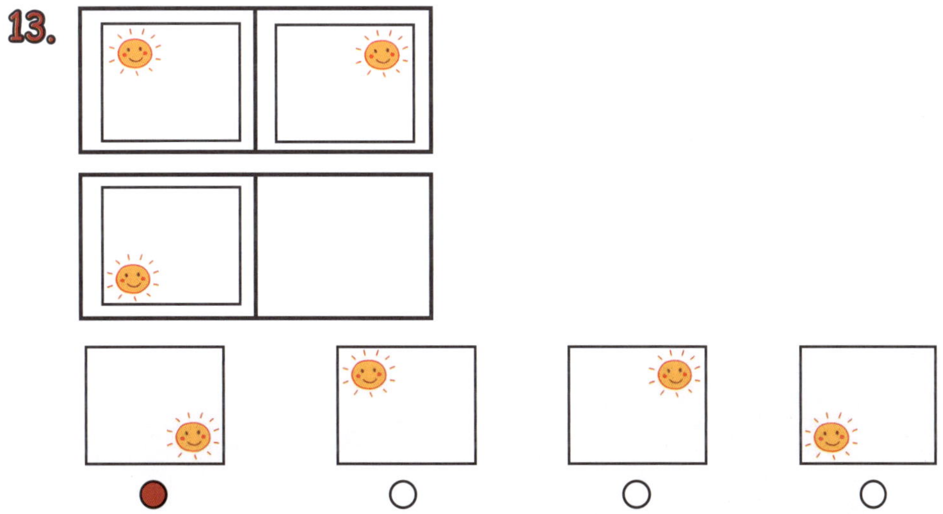

Mark the circle under the picture that belongs in the empty box.

In the top boxes, the sun starts in the top corner and then moves to the other top corner.

In the bottom boxes, the sun moves in the same way, from one bottom corner to the other. The sun's moving in the same way, only in a different part of the square.

14.

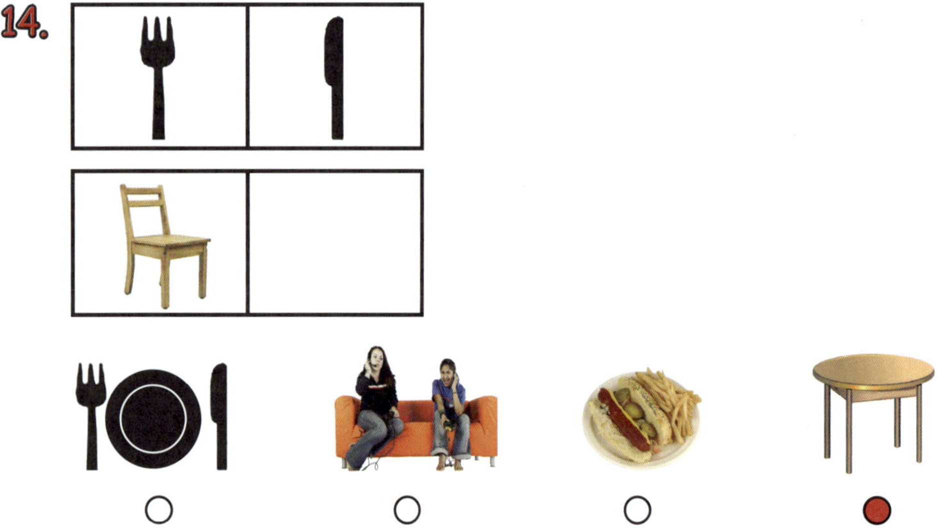

Now try number 14, the last one. Mark the circle under the picture that belongs in the empty box.

In the top boxes, there's a knife and a fork. You sometimes use a knife and a fork together.

In the bottom boxes, there's a chair and an empty box. Is there a picture of something that you sometimes use with a chair? A table.

Usually, you use a fork and knife together, and also a chair and table together.

Section VII
Arithmetic Reasoning

Even if children are too young to be formally taught complex arithmetic, such as division and fractions, they nevertheless probably have an implicit understanding of these concepts. For example, if you show a young child six cookies, and say that you will be sharing them equally, the child will be sure to get his or her share.

This section will familiarize children with the reasoning that underlies the following basic arithmetic functions: counting and relative amounts, addition, subtraction, multiplication, division, and fractions.

1.

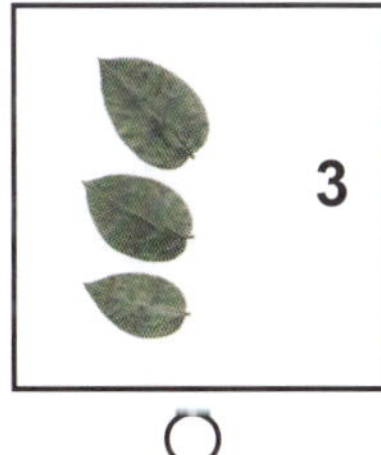

Look at the pictures in the number 1. There are four pictures of things and a number that goes with it. One of these pictures has a mistake. Mark the circle under the picture that has a mistake.

Let's look at each picture and count what's in it. Is the number next to it the same as the number of things in the picture? In the first picture, there's one thing, but it has the number 2 next to it. Go ahead and mark the circle under that picture if you haven't done so already.

2.

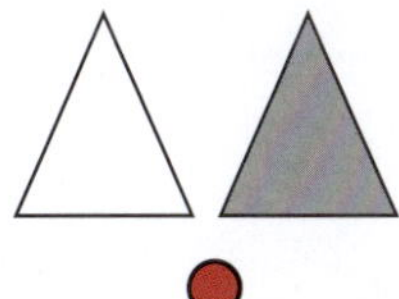

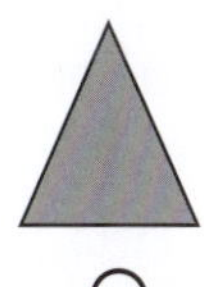

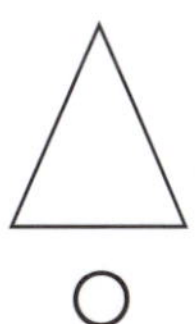

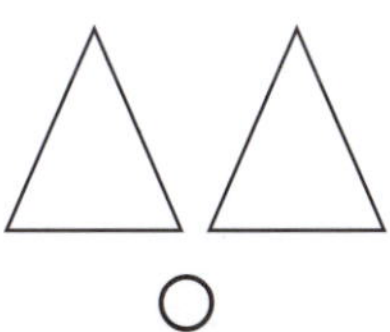

Look at the triangles in number 2. Mark the circle under the picture that shows TWO triangles and ONE of them is gray.

Let's take it one step at a time. First, find the pictures with TWO triangles and circle them. Next, find the one you circled which has only one gray triangle.

3.

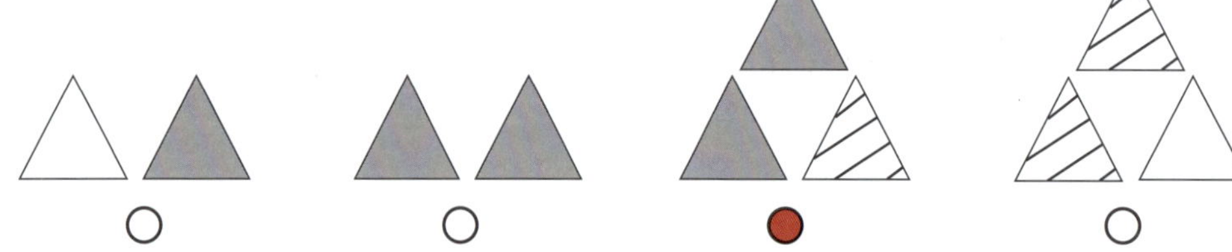

Look at the pictures in number 3. These triangles are a little different. Mark the circle under the picture that shows THREE triangles and TWO of them are gray.

Let's take it one step at a time. First, circle the ones with THREE triangles. Next, find the one you've circled which has two gray triangles.

You're paying careful attention and that's great.

4.

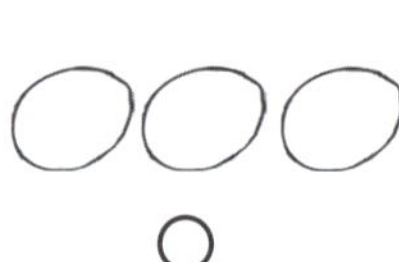
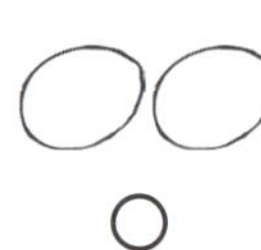
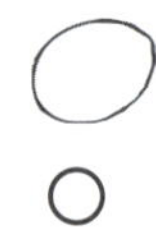

Look at the nest in number 4. It can fit only three eggs in it at a time. Mark the circle under the picture that shows TOO MANY eggs for this nest to hold.

We know the nest cannot hold more than three eggs. Which picture shows more than three eggs? You can change your answer if you thought carefully and changed your mind.

5.

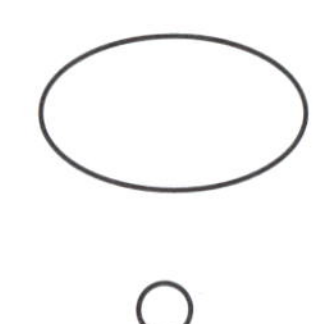
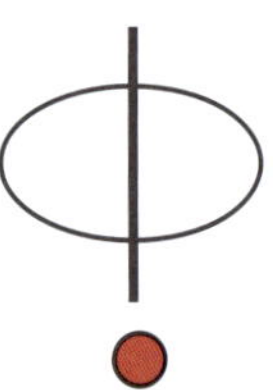
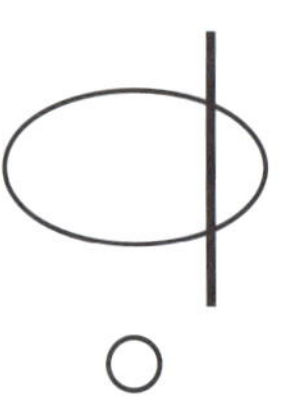
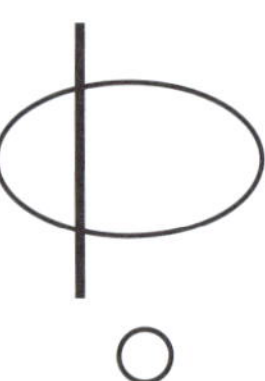

Mark the circle under the picture that shows an oval that is cut in HALF.

I think you might already know something important. When something is cut in half, one half looks just like the other half. The second one is the one that's cut in half because both sides look exactly the same.

6.

Mark the circle under the picture that shows the bear HALFWAY IN-BETWEEN the two balls.

If something is halfway in-between two things, that means that it is in the middle. When something is in the middle, there is the same amount of space on both sides of it.

7.

Let's move on to number 7. This is a picture of a boy named Sammy and his mom. Sammy and his mom had eight strawberries to share. Sammy's mom gave him HALF of the strawberries. Mark the circle under the picture that shows how many strawberries Sammy got.

Let's look at the strawberries next to Sammy and his mom. If something is divided in half, there is the same amount in both of the halves. Let's count how many strawberries are next to Sammy and his mom. There are eight.

Now let's divide these eight strawberries in half. Draw a line right down the middle of this group of eight strawberries. On one side of the line, we have four strawberries. On the other side of the line, we have the same number. So if Sammy got what was on one side of the line, he got four strawberries. Go ahead and mark the circle under the picture that shows four strawberries, if you haven't already.

8.

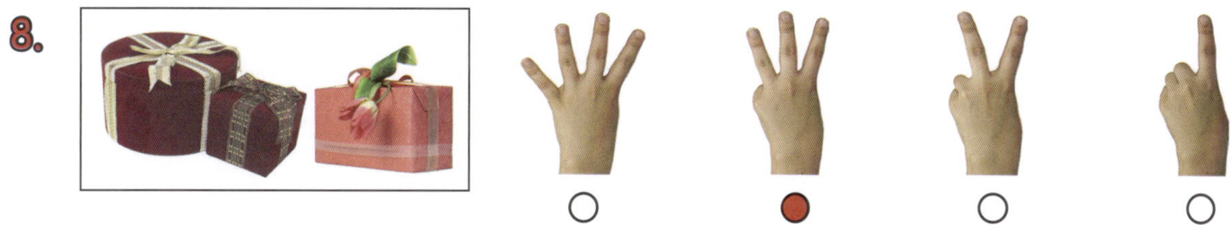

Let's move on to number 8, which is about the presents that a girl named Rosa got for her birthday. She was excited about getting presents. She used her fingers to count all of the presents that she was getting. She got TWO presents from her grandma, and ONE present from her uncle. Mark the circle under the picture of the hand that shows how many presents Rosa counted altogether.

Rosa counted TWO presents from her grandma and ONE from her uncle. Here we have a picture with two presents and then one more present. The first two are from her grandma, and the last one is from her uncle. So how many are there altogether? If Rosa counted three presents altogether, which hand shows her counting to three? The second one.

These exercises are getting a little harder now. No one expects you to get them all right. As long as you think carefully and take your time you're doing a good job.

9.

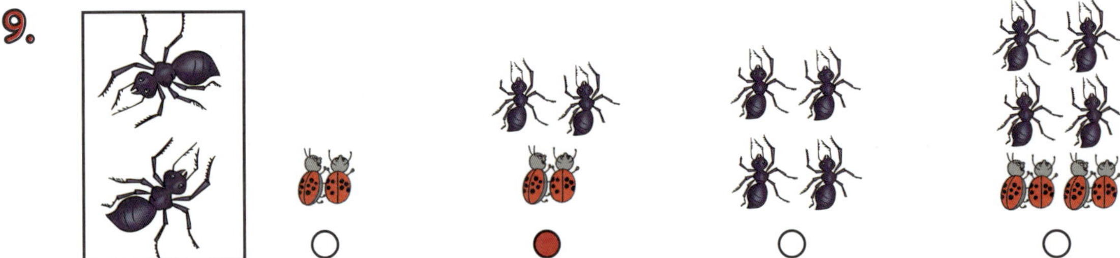

Look at the bugs in number 9. The TWO ants invited TWO ladybugs to a picnic. Mark the circle under the picture that shows ALL the bugs that will be at the picnic.

Two ants and two ladybugs are four bugs altogether. Which picture shows two ants and two ladybugs? It's the second picture.

10.

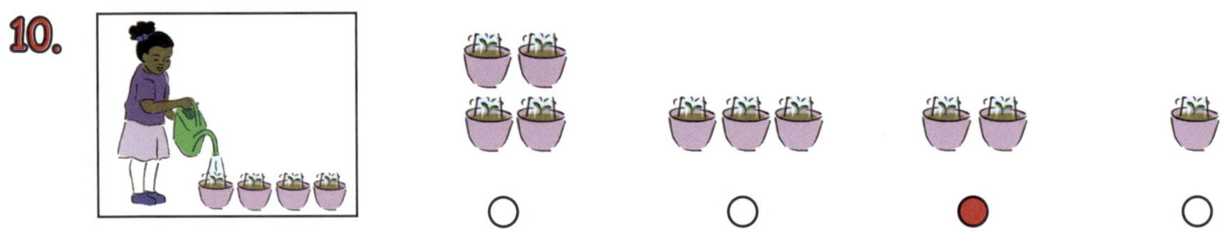

Let's move on to number 10. It shows a girl named April who is watering her FOUR plants. April gave water to TWO of her plants. After she watered two of them, she ran out of water. Mark the circle under the picture that shows the plants that did NOT get water.

Let's look at the picture of April and her plants. She gave two of her plants water. If you put your finger over two of the plants that already got water, how many plants are left that did NOT get water? There are two.

11.

Let's look at the horses in number 11. Claire visited a ranch with horses. She had FIVE carrots in her bag. The horses ate only THREE of her carrots. Mark the circle under the picture that shows the number of carrots that were left in Claire's bag.

Let's look at the top picture of the horses and the carrots. Let's say that the first horse ate the first carrot. Let's cross out one horse and one carrot. Let's say that the second horse got the second carrot, and cross out one more horse and one more carrot. Now, let's say that the third horse ate the third carrot, and cross out one more carrot and the last horse. How many carrots are left?

Some of these will be easy for you, but some will be more difficult. I'm proud of you because you're really trying.

12.

Let's move on to number 12. Jada needed a new pair of boots. She tried on TWO PAIRS of boots to make sure that her mother bought her the right size. Which of these pictures shows TWO PAIRS of boots?

One pair of boots is two boots. If you have on one pair of boots, then you have two boots. This can be tricky. But stay with it and you'll get it. If you have on a pair of boots, how many boots do you have again? Two. If you have two pairs, then you have four boots altogether. The second picture is the right one.

You've completed the essential exercises in the Arithmetic Reasoning section. Continue with the remaining exercises only if the previous ones were easily completed.

13.

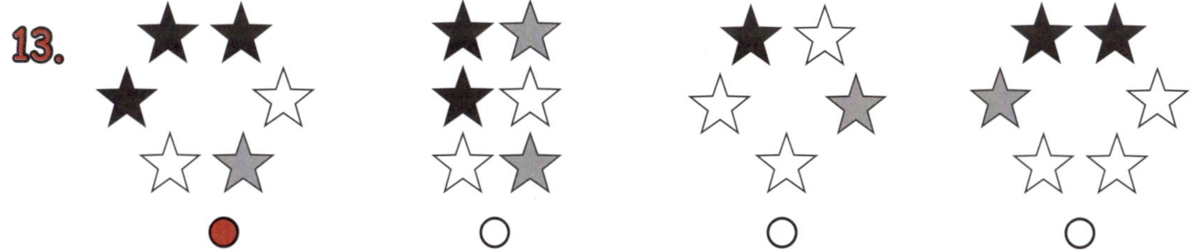

Look at the stars in number 13. Mark the circle under the picture that shows half of the stars are black.

Let's look at the first choice. If you put your finger over the stars that are NOT black, you see only three black stars. The three stars that are black look just like the other three stars, except the color is different. How many stars are there in this first group of stars? Six. How many of those six stars are black? Three. Half of six is three. The first choice is correct.

14.

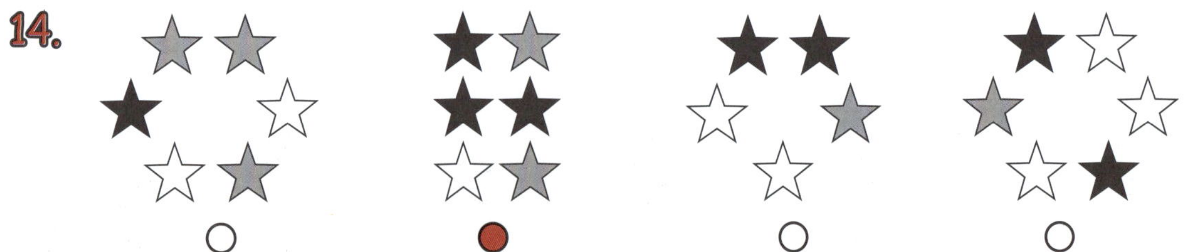

Let's move on to 14. This next one is a little different from the one you just did. Mark the circle under the picture that shows half of the stars are black.

This time, the second choice is correct. Here, there are six stars, and three of them are black. This one is tricky because the three black stars are not all together. But still, three is always half of six.

15.

2 3 4 6

Look at the pictures in number 15. Jamie, Chris, and Danny are friends. An older boy gives them 12 little toy cars that he doesn't play with any more. The top picture shows the boys and the 12 cars that they were given.

Jamie, Chris, and Danny decide that they are each going to take home the same number of cars. Mark the circle under the number of cars that each boy takes home.

There are three children who take home the cars. Let's say Jamie gets the first car in the row of cars at the top. Write the letter "J" over that first car. Chris gets the second car, so you can write the letter "C" over the second car. Danny gets the third car, so you can write the letter "D" over the third car.

Now, let's look at the cars that have the letter "J" for Jamie over them. All the cars in this first column belong to Jamie. Let's count them. There are 4. Now let's see how many cars belong to Chris and Danny. There are 4.

Now, how many cars does each of the friends take home? It took a little time to figure it out, but you did it.

16.

Number 16 is about a monkey named Sampson, who loves to eat bananas and apples. Every time Sampson eats ONE apple, he eats TWO bananas. One day for lunch, Sampson ate TWO apples. Mark the circle under the picture that shows how many apples and bananas he ate.

Every time Sampson eats one apple, he eats two bananas to go along with it. This means that every time you see one apple, you should see two bananas to go along with that apple. Let's go through all the choices.

Let's start with the first choice. If you look at the first apple, there are two bananas underneath it. Now, our rule is that every time you see ONE apple, you should see TWO bananas. Does this go by our rule? It does. The second apple also has two bananas underneath it. Does this go by our rule? It does.

Let's look at the other choices. Remember, each time you see one apple, there should be two bananas underneath it. Do the other choices go by this rule? No.

17.

4 ○ 6 ○ 7 ● 9 ○

In number 17, Mr Jensen fixes bikes. He has TWO bicycles that he needs to fix today. He also needs to fix ONE tricycle. Every bicycle has two tires, and the tricycle has three. He changes ALL the tires on the bicycles and tricycle. Mark the circle under the number of new tires he will need

First, let's count all the tires that he will need for the two bicycles. If he has two bicycles, he will need four tires.

Next, let's count all the tires that he will need for the tricycle. The tricycle has three tires. Now we add the four bicycle tires with the three tricycle tires and we find out how many tires Mr. Jensen needs.

Section VIII

Sequencing

A sequence is a series of pictures or events that follows a pattern or a logical order. The key to understanding sequences is being able to predict what will come next. The four types of sequences that will be shown in this section are sequences that:

1. fit a rhythmic pattern (red, then white, then red, then white, and so on),
2. show movement (e.g., a ball rotating position),
3. increase or decrease in size, number, or some other characteristic; or
4. tell a story.

This section requires children not just to predict the sequence, but also to verbalize the sequence so that they can build confidence in predicting what comes next.

Right now, we're going to be looking at some things, and we're going to PREDICT what comes next. PREDICTING is when you figure out what's going to happen before it happens. We're going to be predicting what comes next in a group of pictures.

1.

Look at the pictures in number 1. Pretty soon, you're going to mark the circle under the picture that comes next, the bunny or the carrot. You may already know what comes next because you're probably very good at predicting.

But right now, we're going to slow down. Before you mark the circle under what comes next, I want you to SAY the pattern with me: bunny-carrot, bunny-carrot, bunny ... Right, it's the carrot that comes next. It's good to say it out loud so that you really know what comes next. Now mark the circle under the carrot.

2.

Let's move on to number 2. We've got a butterfly, a frog, and a bee. Let's say it out loud. Butterfly, frog, bee, butterfly, frog, bee ... Now mark the circle under what comes next. It's the butterfly.

3.

Now look at the pictures in number 3. Mark the circle under the picture that belongs in the empty box.

We've got a fish and a crab. Let's say it out loud. Fish, crab, fish, crab, fish ... Now mark the circle under what comes next. It's the crab.

What do all these creatures in number 3 have in common? How are they alike? They are all sea creatures.

4.

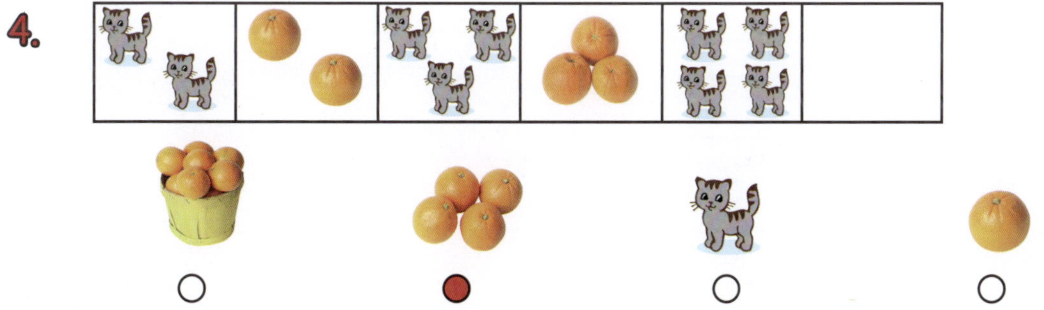

Let's move on to number 4. Mark the circle under the picture that comes next.

Let's say it out loud. Two cats, two oranges, three cats, three oranges, four cats, four oranges. You might think that the right answer is the bucket of oranges, but four oranges is the better answer. Remember, you can change your answer if you've thought carefully and you changed your mind.

5.

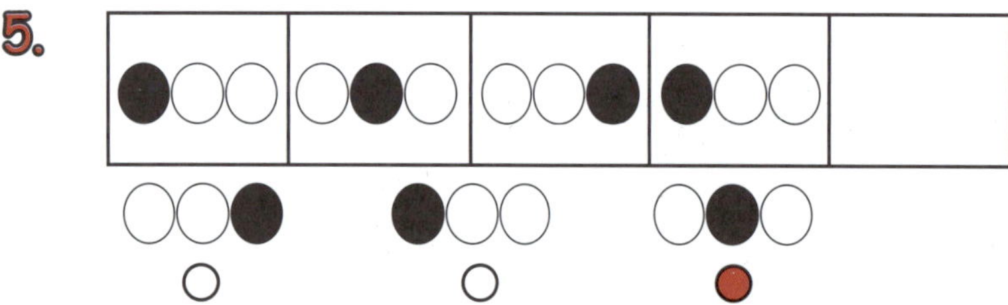

Now we're on number 5. Here are some circles in groups of three. Mark the circle under the group that you think comes next.

Here, the black circle is moving. It's moving across the row. First it's in the first position. Then, it moves to the middle. Finally, it moves all the way to the end. Then it starts over again.

Before the empty box, the black circle is in the first position. If we know that the black circle is moving across the row, then the answer to mark is the last one, with the black circle in the middle.

6.

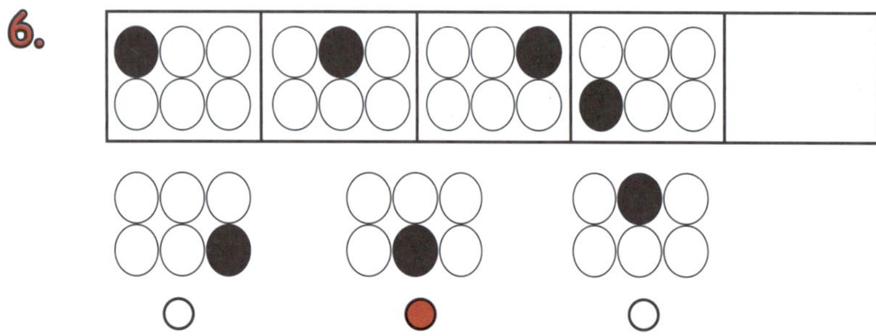

Look at number 6, and mark the circle under the group that comes next in the sequence.

Here, the black circle is moving across TWO rows. First, it moves across the first row. Then, it moves down to the second row and moves across that row.

The one that comes next is the second answer, because the black circle is moving across the second row and is now in the middle of that row.

7.

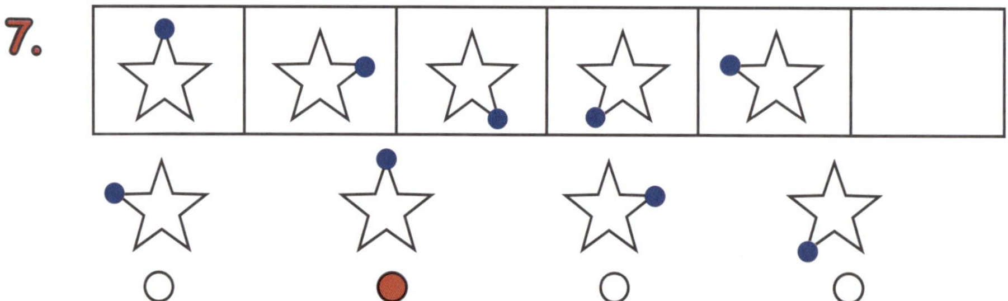

Now let's look at number 7. The little ball is moving around the points of the star. Mark the circle under the star that shows where the ball will be next.

The ball is moving around all the points of the star. In the first picture, the ball is way up top. In the second picture, it moves down to the next point of the star. Let's look at all the pictures so that we can predict where the ball will be next.

8.

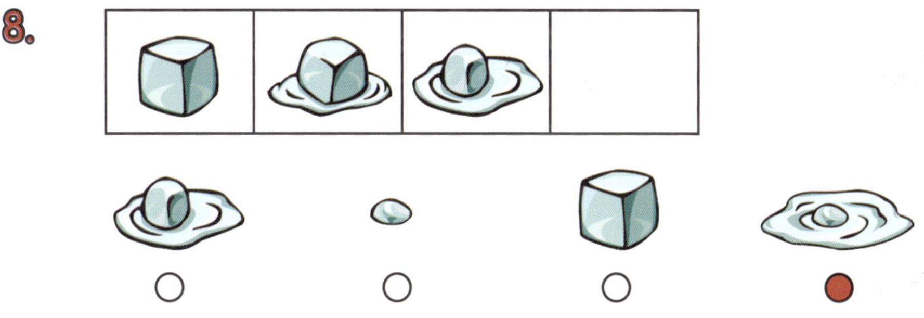

Look at number 8 with the ice cube. Mark the circle under the picture that comes next.

It's melting and melting. It cannot be the first choice because when something melts, it doesn't stay the same. Let's cross out the first choice.

Now let's look at the third choice. It can't be the third choice because it looks like the whole ice cube hasn't melted. Cross out the third choice. Now we have two more left. The second choice would be okay, but when something melts there should be liquid around it. The last choice is still melting and about the right size, so it's the best answer.

9.

For number 9, I'm going to tell you a story. The story has a beginning, a middle, and an end. After I read the story, mark the circle beside the set of pictures that shows what happens in the story. Ready? Here's the story.

> When there's a fire, Firefighter Bill works very hard. First, he carries the big hose on his shoulder. Then he puts the hose into the fire hydrant and TURNS the fire hydrant on. Finally, the water is SPRAYED from the hose so that he can put the fire out.

I'll read the story again so you can check your answer.* It's the first set of pictures that tells the story.

**Repeat the story above.*

10.

In number 10, the set of pictures tells a story about a girl named Sarah who did something very silly with a birthday cake. You don't need words to understand this story. Look at the pictures and mark the circle beside the group of pictures that tells the story.

Sarah is really very silly. One thing we know that she did is put her face in the cake! After she put her face in the cake, she was covered with cake. The first set of pictures tells the story.

The second and third sets of pictures do not tell the story at all. After she puts her face in the cake, she must have cake on her face. Also, after she puts her face in the cake, her cake is ruined and cannot be whole. So that's why the first choice is the only one that tells the story.

You've completed the essential exercises in the Sequencing section. Continue with the remaining exercises only if the previous ones were easily completed.

11.

Now we're on number 11. This puzzle is a bit different. Later I'm going to tell you a secret about how to figure this out, but now I want you to try it by yourself. Mark the circle under the shape that you think comes next. Take a guess if you don't know.

Even most adults are challenged by number 11. Let's move on to number 12.

12.

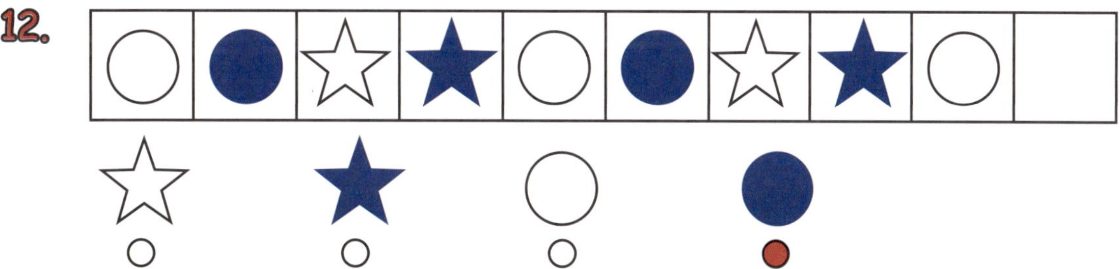

After we're through with this one, you'll have learned a secret that you can use to see if your answer for number 11 was right. The secret is to break it down into steps and take it one step at a time.

There are blue and white circles and stars. First, let's figure out what COLOR comes next. It goes white, blue, white, blue ... What color comes next? Blue.

Now let's figure out what SHAPE comes next. It goes circle, circle, star, star, circle, circle, star, star, ... What shape comes next? A circle. We know that what comes next is a blue circle. Go ahead and mark it.

13.

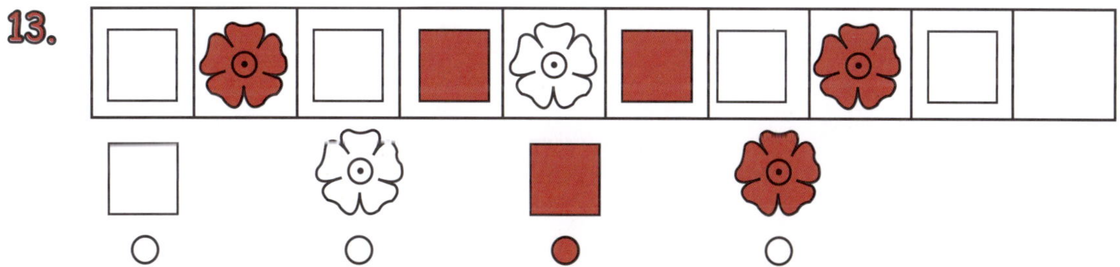

Number 13, is the same as number 11. This time, I want you to figure it out in two steps. First, figure out what color comes next. Then, figure out what shape comes next. Say the pattern out loud (quietly) to yourself. Go ahead and mark the circle under what comes next.

This one is tricky because the color goes from white to red and the shapes have their own pattern too. First, let's try to figure out what COLOR comes next. It goes white, red, white, red ... What color comes next? Red. Now let's figure out what SHAPE comes next. Square, flower, square, square, flower, square, square, flower, square ... What shape comes next? A square.

14.

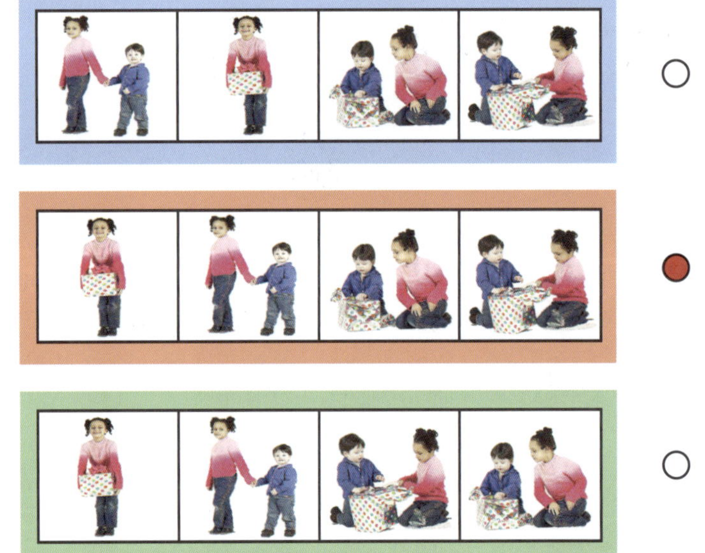

Number 14 is another story about Sarah. Mark the circle next to the set of pictures that show's the order of the story.

> Sarah's little brother had a birthday party. Sarah was very curious about one of her brother's presents. FIRST, she picked up the present to see how heavy it was. THEN, she decided to get her brother. She took her brother by the hand and brought him over to the present so that he could open it himself. But her brother was younger, and he was taking a long time to unwrap it himself. So, FINALLY, Sarah decided to help her brother unwrap the present.

We know that the first thing Sarah does is pick up the present. We can cross out the answer that does NOT show her picking up the present first.

That leaves us with two choices. We know that Sarah lets her brother open the gift himself first, but, finally, Sarah helps him unwrap the present. Which one of these shows Sarah letting her brother open it by himself first, before she finally joins in to help him?

15.

Now we're on #15, the last problem in this section. What do you think was inside the present that Sarah's little brother unwrapped? Try to predict by marking the circle under what might be inside the present.

First of all, is there anything that is too big to fit inside the box? The tricycle. Cross it out. Now, is there anything that shouldn't be kept in a box? The dog. Cross that out, too. That leaves us with the fire truck and the candies. The candies can fit inside the box, but they're actually too small for that big box. That leaves us with the fire truck. I'll bet Sarah's brother got a fire truck for his birthday.

Section IX
Recognizing Patterns

In this section, children will demonstrate their ability to recognize patterns. In order to do this, they will see that a piece of the pattern is missing and then will figure out which of the four choices is the missing piece. When children find the missing piece of the pattern, they show their ability to recognize that pattern.

Discussions in this section encourage children to explain why the missing piece fits the pattern. This can strengthen their understanding of the order and symmetry in patterns, and hone their visual recognition skills.

1.

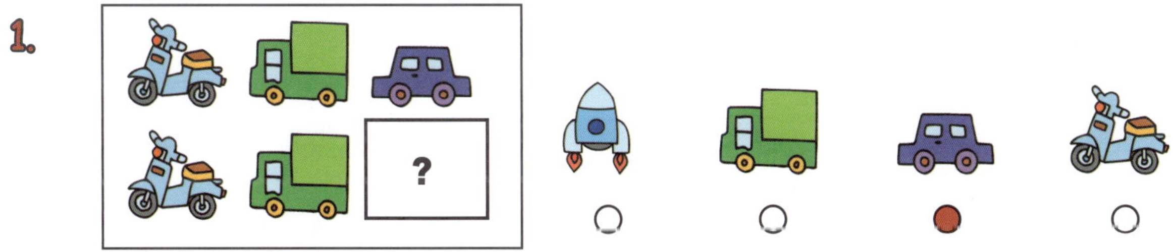

Now we're going to do some work where your job is to figure out what's missing. You'll see a picture where there's some important part missing. The part that's missing will be covered by a white rectangle with a question mark inside. Now, look at number 1. See the rectangle with a question mark?

I want you to mark the circle under the vehicle that belongs in the rectangle's place.

I want to tell you something important that you probably already know. In order to figure out what's missing, you have to look at EVERYTHING ELSE in the picture and see how things go together. In this picture, every vehicle is just like the one that's above it.

You can see there are two motorcycles, and the one above is just like the one below. Then there are two trucks, and each one is the same. So when you see the car that is right above the rectangle, you know that the thing that's missing is another car. Remember that you can change your answer after thinking it over.

2.

Look at the picture in number 2. Mark the circle under the part of the picture that's missing.

It's still the car that's missing. Sometimes, there are lots of things going on in a picture. Some of the things going on are important and some are not important. This picture is a lot like the one before, except in this one, there are motorcycles all around the other vehicles. The car is still the part that's missing.

3.

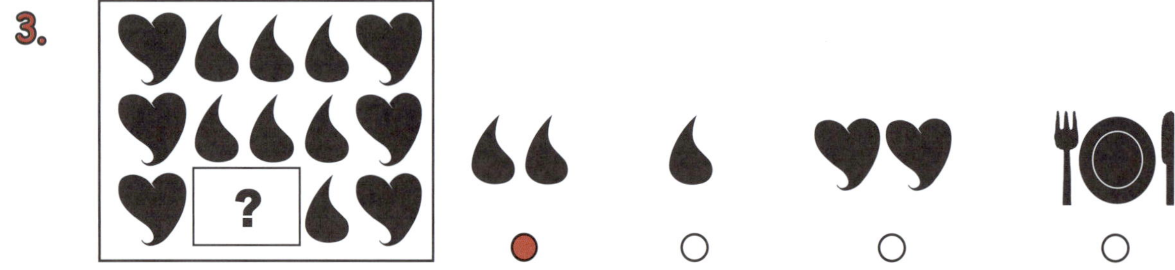

Number 3 also has an important part missing. Go ahead and mark the circle under the part of the picture that's missing.

To figure out what's missing, we have to look at the whole picture. There's no fork, plate, and spoon in the pattern, so you can cross that choice out. You can see how there are two raindrops right above the rectangle. So that's why the raindrops are the part that's missing.

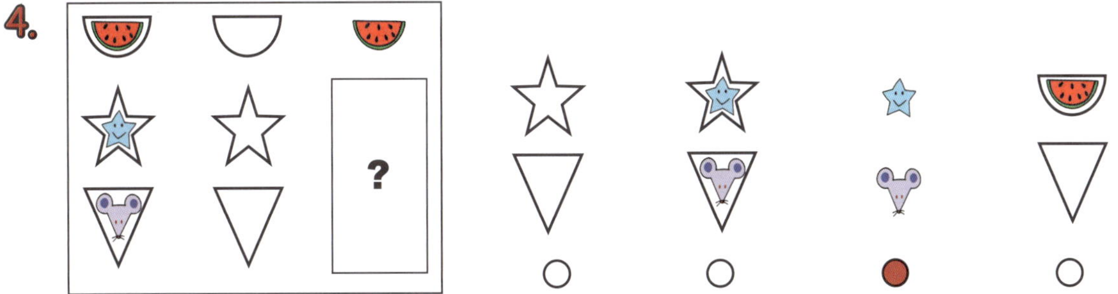

Let's move on to number 4. Mark the circle under the part of the picture that's missing.

To figure out what's missing, we have to look at the whole picture. Let's start with the first row. There's a watermelon inside a shape, then there's the shape by itself, and finally the watermelon all by itself. In the second row, there's a star face inside a star shape, then a shape of a star. What do you think comes next? The star face by itself.

Now, in the last row, there's a mouse inside a shape. Then there's the shape by itself. What comes next in this row? The mouse by itself.

Now, we have to put things together. We're looking for the star face by itself in the second row, and then the mouse by itself in the third row. Mark the circle under the part of the picture that's missing, if you haven't already.

Now let's move on to number 5, with the ladybug. Mark the circle under the part of the picture that's missing.

To figure out what's missing, we have to look at the whole picture. Here, the ladybug is traveling. The arrows show where the ladybug is going. So mark the circle under the arrow that shows the direction the ladybug is traveling in the rectangle.

6.

In number 6, mark the circle under the picture that is missing.

Why did you pick that one? The circles in the middle and corners are all the same.

Now let's look at all of the pointing arrows. They are all pointing in different directions. Now which arrow completes the picture by pointing in a different direction?

7.

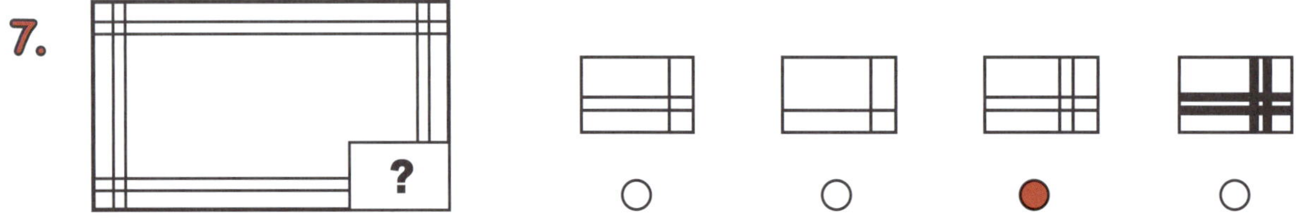

Now we're on number 7. Mark the circle under the part of the picture that's missing.

In this picture, there are four lines going down and four lines going across. In the corners of the picture, two lines cross. When we look at the choices, we've got to pick one where two lines cross each other. In the first choice, there are two lines going across, but there's only one line going down, so cross it out.

In the second choice, there's only one line going down and one line going across. So that's not it. Cross it out.

The third choice has two lines going down and two lines going across, just like in the rest of the picture. So that's it. The last choice has two lines going down and two lines going across, but those lines are not like the lines in the picture. You can change your answer after thinking it over.

8.

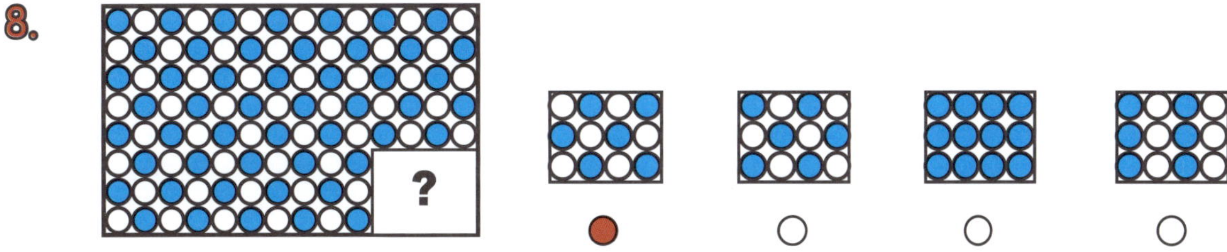

In number 8, mark the circle under the part of the picture that's missing.

To figure out what's missing, we have to look carefully at the big picture. This picture is a bunch of blue and white dots. They are not all blue dots, so cross out the third choice that shows all blue dots. They also are not arranged in stripes, so cross out the last choice that shows stripes.

The answer is either the first choice or the second choice. If you look again at the big picture, a circle is never next to a circle of the same color. The second choice would make two blue dots right next to each other. The first choice is the right one.

9.

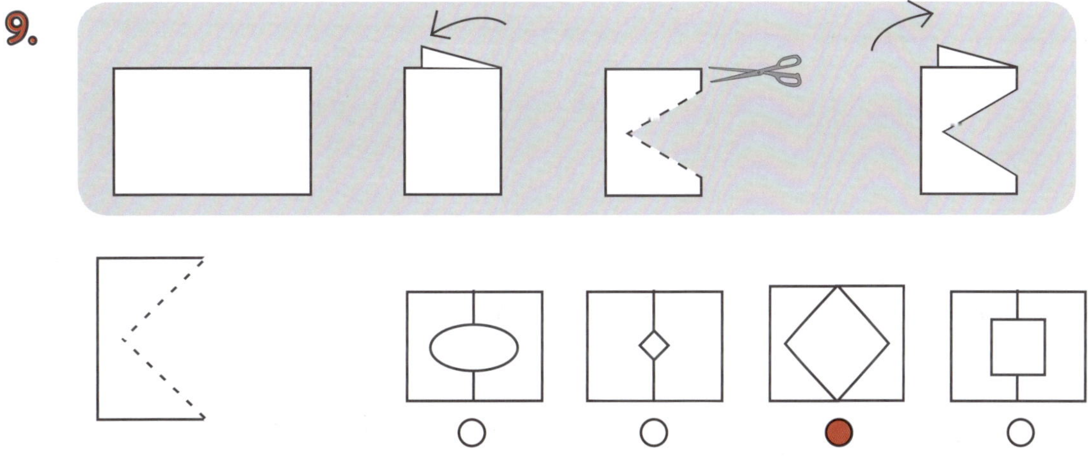

Number 9 is different from the others you've done. I'll tell you how it works. First, I want you to imagine that I have a plain piece of paper, then fold that piece in half. Now imagine that I take scissors and cut out a piece of it. Finally, I unfold the paper. What will it look like? Mark the circle under the picture of what the opened paper will look like.

If the folded paper is cut in half, one half looks just like the other half. *(e.g., #5 Arithmetic Reasoning* section where the oval is cut in half.*)* This is called symmetry.

When we look at what's cut out of the picture, we see a triangle. The first choice is an oval, so we know that's not it, and we can cross it out. The last choice does not match the cut out, so we know that's not it either. The second choice is in the same shape as the cutout, but it's too small. The third shape looks exactly like both halves of the cutout. So the third choice is correct.

10. 

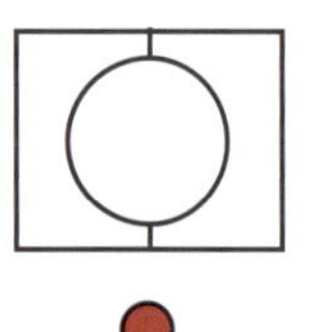 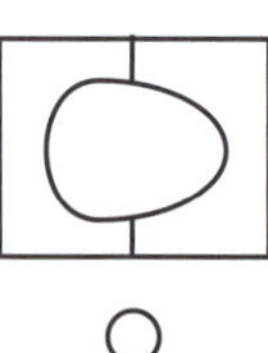 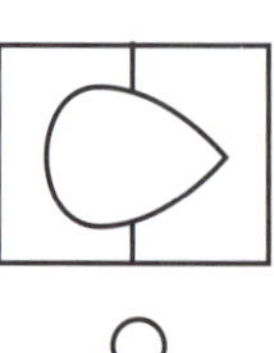 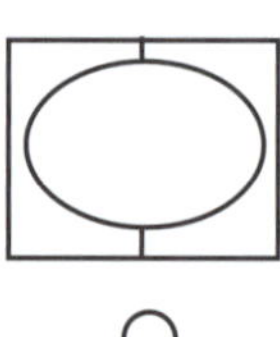

Number 10 works just like number 9. Mark the circle under the picture of what the opened paper will look like.

Remember that one half of the picture must look just like the other half. Let's look at the choices. The first choice looks just like both halves put together.

The second choice has one half that doesn't look like the other half. The third choice also has one half that doesn't look like the other half. The last choice has both halves that look alike, but they're too big. So the first choice is the best answer.

You've completed the essential exercises in the Recognizing Patterns section. Continue with the remaining exercises only if the previous ones were easily completed.

11. 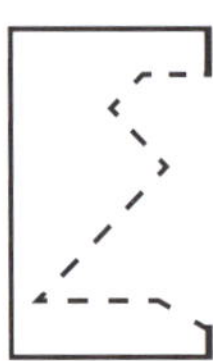

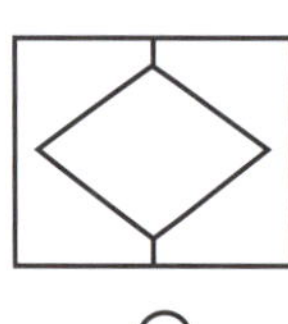 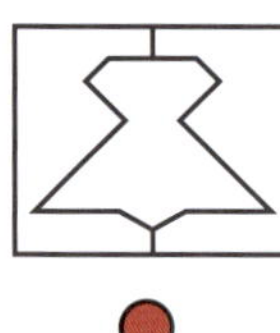 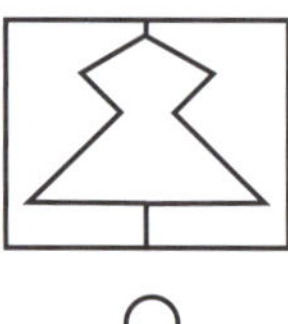 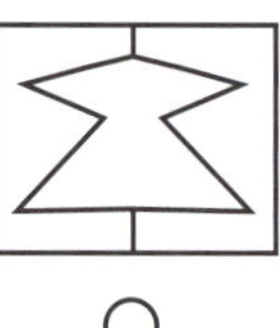

We're on number 11. This paper cutout is very challenging. Go ahead and mark the circle under the picture that shows what the opened paper will look like.

Let's look at the first one. It does not match, so we can cross it out. The second one looks like it might be right, but we'll need to compare it with the third and fourth one.

If you look carefully at the lines, you can see that the third and fourth choices have straight lines on the bottom. But the folded paper has a bump in the line on the bottom. If you look carefully, you can see that the second choice is what the opened paper will look like.

Tell me, was that a tough one to figure out? If so, good for you that you kept trying.

12.

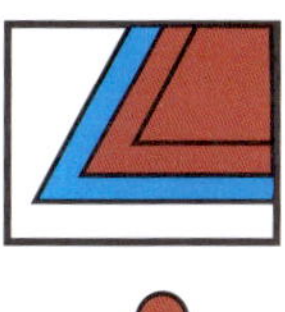

Now look at the triangles in number 12. Mark the circle under the part of the pattern that's missing.

This is a tricky one. There are three triangles that overlap. The lowest triangle is blue, the next triangle is red, and the triangle on top is see-through. So it's the same color as whatever's underneath it. So the second choice is correct.

Let's look at the first choice because that's a tricky one. The top triangle is white. It's easy to make the mistake of thinking that the top triangle is white.

13.

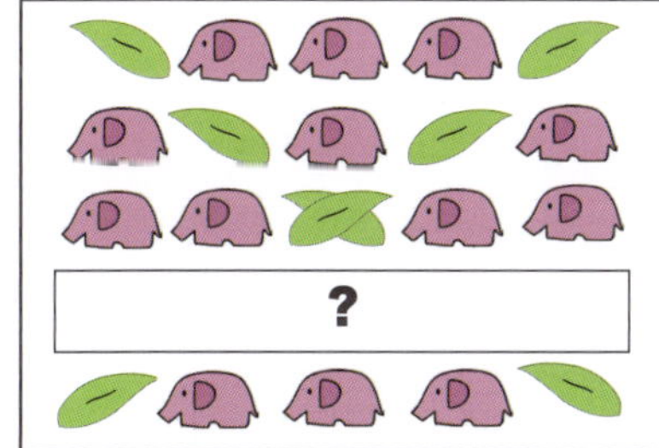
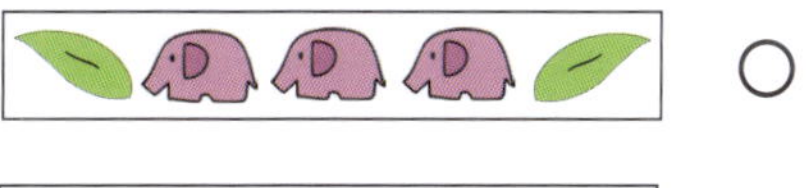
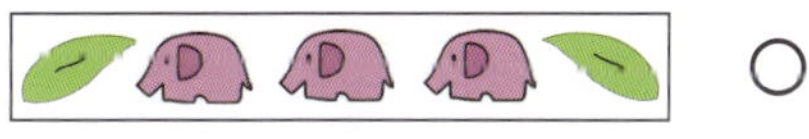
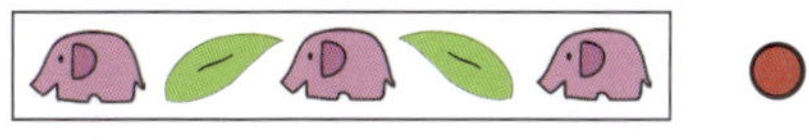

Look at the elephants in number 13. Mark the circle beside the part of the pattern that's missing.

There are a bunch of elephants, and also green leaves that make an "X" in the middle of the pattern. Let's look at the "X" in the middle of the pattern. I want you to take your pencil and draw an "X" where the leaves are. When you draw the "X" you can see where the leaves should go in the missing part of the pattern. It looks like the first thing in the missing row should be an elephant. The second thing should be a leaf. You can see that the line you drew when you connected the leaves shows us where the leaf should go. Our "X" also shows us the direction that the leaf should be pointing. It looks like the best fit would be the third choice. That's where the leaves look most like the part of the "X" that's missing.

14.

Now this one, number 14, may be a challenge. Give it a try, and then we can discuss it. Look it over carefully and mark the circle under the piece that is missing.

If you look at the pattern, it's as if each thing takes its place in line going first. If you look at the first row, the striped ball is first, then the rings, then the red ball, and then the happy face.

Next the happy face moves into the first place and "bumps" all the other things down the line. So now the happy face is first, then the striped ball, then the rings, and finally the red ball. Now that we know how this pattern works, we can figure out the missing piece of the pattern.

Which thing is supposed to have its turn going first? The red ball. Now that we know that everything else just moves down the line, we know that the happy face comes next, and then the striped ball, and finally the rings. Go ahead and mark the circle beside that missing piece.